This journal belongs to

....

3-MINUTE DEVOTIONS

FOR WOMEN

JOURNAL

© 2017 by Barbour Publishing, Inc.

Print ISBN 978-1-68322-205-7

Published by Barbour Books, an imprint of Barbour Publishing, Inc., P.O. Box 719, Uhrichsville, Ohio 44683, www.barbourbooks.com

Our mission is to publish and distribute inspirational products offering exceptional value and biblical encouragement to the masses.

Member of the
Evangelical Christian
Publishers Association

Printed in China.

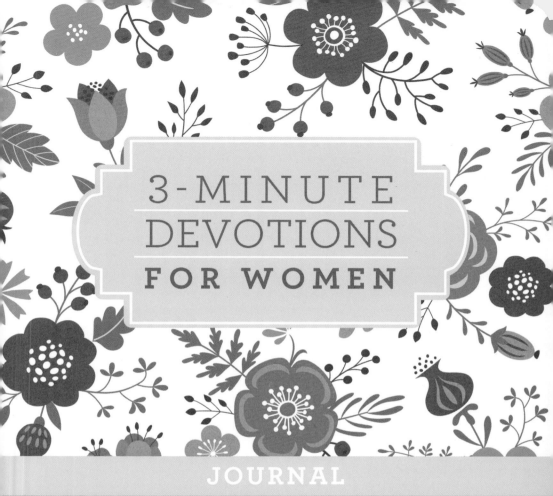

3-MINUTE
DEVOTIONS
FOR WOMEN

JOURNAL

BARBOUR BOOKS
An Imprint of Barbour Publishing, Inc.

BE STILL AND LEARN

But his delight is in the law of the LORD, and in His law he meditates day and night.
PSALM 1:2 NKJV

Quiet time to learn of God's ways requires discipline. Yet our daily routine cries for our attention. We find ourselves with too much to do—and the ticking of the clock constantly in our ears.

Our loved ones cannot be ignored. Duty calls. There are meals to prepare, medicine to dispense, and clothes to arrange. When is there time for God?

It's easy to put our quiet time with God on the back burner. But the very thing we need most—hope—only the Lord can provide. He understands our exhaustion and frustration. He feels our pain and sadness. He's waiting to extend grace when we call upon Him.

Our quiet time—reading scripture and praying—is like water on a sponge. It fills us and expands our ability to keep going. It strengthens us for the day. It empowers us to fulfill what God requires.

Don't let the call of your duties drown out the need for quiet time. Discipline yourself to set aside a few minutes for the Lord. He is our hope, our salvation. We need His fellowship. To neglect that time is dangerous.

*Father, help me to focus on You, to carve out minutes from my day
to spend in prayer and the Word. My desire is to fellowship with You.*

WHO HELPS THE HELPER?

*The LORD is my strength and my shield; my heart trusted in him, and I am helped:
therefore my heart greatly rejoiceth; and with my song will I praise him.*
PSALM 28:7 KJV

Women tend to be helpers. They can't help it.

God made them that way. From the foundation of the earth, their primary job has been to help.

It is a woman's nature to assist, to nurture, to render care. Even in these days of more "equitable" roles, it is typically the woman who is found feeding the baby at 2:00 a.m., cheering the young soccer players, counseling the college student by long-distance phone calls, holding a shaky hand in a hospital room, and comforting the bereaved at a funeral.

Helping can be exhausting. The needs of young children, teens, grandchildren, and aging parents can stretch us—women and men both—until we're ready to snap. And then we find that *we* need help.

Who helps the helper?

The Lord does. When we are weak, He is strong. When we are vulnerable, He is our shield. When we can no longer trust in our own resources, we can trust in Him.

And we can trust Him before we snap. He is always there, ready to help.

Rejoice in Him, praise His name, and you will find the strength to go on.

Father, I'm worn out. I can't care for all the people and needs You bring into my life by myself. I need Your strength. Thank You for being my helper and my shield.

I'M NOT CRAZY AFTER ALL

We have this hope as an anchor for the soul, firm and secure.
HEBREWS 6:19 NIV

Am I going crazy? Am I the only person who feels this way? As we go through life, it seems like we occasionally lose our minds.

The challenge of balancing schedules, dealing with demanding personalities, and maintaining relationships and friendships can drive our entire life off course. Like a ship tossed in a storm, we can drift in a strange sea, overcome by uncontrollable waves.

But we do have an anchor—our hope in God. What does an anchor do? It prevents drifting by attaching firmly to the unmoving floor of the sea. God is that seabed, firm and secure, and Jesus is the anchor connecting us to the Father. Our anchor of hope is deep within the seabed of God.

The shape of an anchor reminds us of the cross. No wonder the first-century Christians used an anchor as a symbol of the cross. We are not adrift. We are securely fastened to God through Jesus.

No, you're not crazy when you feel lost and confused. We'll have stormy times—but we are held firm and secure by the anchor of hope.

Lord, I cling to You as my anchor. Although I may feel lost at times,
I know You are here with me, holding me secure, giving me hope.

LABOR OF LOVE

Go to work in the morning and stick to it until evening without watching the clock.
You never know from moment to moment how your work will turn out in the end.
ECCLESIASTES 11:6 MSG

Have you ever had a job where the work was so routine that you were bored, watching the clock, willing the shift to end so you could get on with something you really enjoyed? Or maybe your job demanded so much of you physically, mentally, or emotionally that when you returned home, you wanted nothing more than to put out a large DO NOT DISTURB sign and "veg out" for the evening. Or perhaps you found yourself counting the days until retirement.

God says that any job, any ministry, is profitable. Don't look at the clock, wishing the time away. If you are too exhausted to reach out with God's love for others, then reevaluate what the Lord would have you do in service for Him. But don't hold out on serving Him because you are too "tired." He gave us His all because of His love. Respond in love for Him and give your all, showing His love to others.

Father, may I find joy in serving You today—because of Your love.

WOE IS ME!

*And he said, I have been very jealous for the LORD God of hosts:
because the children of Israel have forsaken thy covenant, thrown down thine
altars, and slain thy prophets with the sword; and I, even I only,
am left; and they seek my life, to take it away.*

1 KINGS 19:14 KJV

Poor Elijah.

The greatest day of his life had turned into the worst. Following a miraculous victory on Mount Carmel as the prophet of the one true God, he had become a sniveling fugitive. Weary of being chased, he sat under a juniper tree, wishing to die.

But God ministered to Elijah, and he went on forty more days to a cave in Mount Horeb.

Still, the prophet pouted. "I've done all this for You, and I'm the only faithful one left. They're chasing me. This isn't fair!"

God met Elijah in his weariness, gave him a new assignment, and assured him that he was not alone. The Lord promised that the situation would be made right.

As God did for Elijah, He'll do for us. If you're feeling weary and overwhelmed as you carry your burden today, don't give up.

Rest in Him. He will nourish you and give you strength for the journey.

God cares for those who care for others.

*Father, if I could find a cave, I'd crawl into it. But I know that's not where
I should be. I know You have greater things for me than what I see
through my tired eyes. Show me the next step and I'll take it.*

SLEEPLESS NIGHTS

In peace I will lie down and sleep, for you alone, Lord, make me dwell in safety.
PSALM 4:8 NIV

When we can't sleep, we squirm and adjust our pillows. Some try to count sheep. Others squint at the clock, calculating the number of hours left until morning—and the amount of sleep they're not getting.

For women, worry and fear are often the cause of insomnia. They plague us at night because the busyness of life that keeps them at bay in the daytime dissipates in the quiet solitude of night. Alone in the dark, it's easy to imagine the worst and feel hopeless about our situations.

But God longs to care for us and give us peace.

Lisa prays out loud when she can't sleep. She says that her fight against worry is a spiritual battle and that audible prayer is a key in winning the fight. Lisa finds rest from the burdens of life when she pictures herself handing her worries to God—and asking Him to hold them until morning.

God never sleeps. He cares for us all night long. We can rest in that care.

Father, help me to trust You in the dark of night. I feel alone and overwhelmed by my many responsibilities. Please give me the gift of peaceful sleep so I can face tomorrow refreshed.

FAMILY COMPLICATIONS

And David said unto him, Fear not: for I will surely shew thee kindness
for Jonathan thy father's sake, and will restore thee all the land of Saul
thy father; and thou shalt eat bread at my table continually.
2 SAMUEL 9:7 KJV

Like people today, Old Testament characters struggled in family relationships. David's wife Michal turned against him. Her father, King Saul, hunted David like an animal, though the younger man ultimately triumphed and was crowned king.

Most rulers executed their opponents—and their families. But King David, in a major risk-taking move, not only returned Saul's estate to his grandson Mephibosheth but also offered him financial support and a place at the king's table.

David's advisors probably thought him crazy. That is, unless they knew Mephibosheth's father, Jonathan. In the midst of family turmoil, he and David were fast friends. Jonathan even offered to step down as Saul's heir and support David's kingship. When his father threatened to kill David, Jonathan risked his own life by defending his friend. Later, Jonathan died with Saul on the battlefield.

David's love for his late friend extended to Jonathan's children. When he summoned Mephibosheth, the terrified man probably thought David was planning to kill him. Instead, the king treated Mephibosheth like a son, welcoming him with open arms.

In our own difficult family situations, loyalty and kindness may also seem an unwise response. But God wants our actions to always reflect His readiness to bless amid heartache and hurt.

Father, help me act in accordance with Your unconditional love.

SPIRITUAL BLESSINGS

Praise be to the God and Father of our Lord Jesus Christ, who has blessed us in the heavenly realms with every spiritual blessing in Christ.
EPHESIANS 1:3 NIV

Discouraged? Dejected? Disillusioned? Sometimes life leaves us feeling downtrodden. Although the Lord has abundantly blessed us, at times it's easy to forget that truth. We may be struggling financially. We may be dealing with marital strife. We may be experiencing health issues. Is it possible to respond with praise when our earthly life appears to conflict with spiritual truth?

Regardless of our circumstances, God has blessed us with every spiritual blessing in Christ. We are not lacking anything in the heavenly realm. The problem is that many times our focus is on the earthly realm. Instead, we can purpose to turn our thoughts heavenward and count the spiritual blessings that are at our disposal. The Lord's indwelling presence guides our minds and comforts our hearts. His resurrection power enables us to persevere triumphantly. His sustaining peace imparts encouragement for today and hope for tomorrow. When we meditate on eternal blessings, our momentary struggles are put into proper perspective. Earthly trials are temporary. Spiritual blessings are forever. Let's embrace the eternal gifts we have been given and praise Him for His abundant provision!

Dear Lord, regardless of my circumstances, help me focus heavenward.
Allow me to praise You for the spiritual blessings I have been given. Amen.

ABIDE IN CHRIST

I am the vine, you are the branches; he who abides in Me and I in him,
he bears much fruit, for apart from Me you can do nothing.
JOHN 15:5 NASB

Do we want the blessing of God on our lives? Of course we do. But how do we obtain it? By abiding in Christ. This means we are to remain, continue, and sink deeper into our relationship with Him. In doing so, we will bear much fruit.

In John 15:12, Jesus inspires us with the words, "Love one another, just as I have loved you" (NASB). That means loving sacrificially, selflessly, totally, regardless of the other person's behavior or how we "feel" each day. When we apply that truth to our lives, we will have an outgrowth of fruitful love we never dreamed possible.

We can be greatly encouraged by reading the entire text of John 15:1–17. Over and over, Jesus tells us to remain or abide in Him. He assures us that apart from Him, we can't do anything. We can't be a good wife, mother, daughter, or sister unless we remain in Christ and seek His will for our lives.

Take time this evening to read through John 15:1–17 slowly and carefully. Think of ways you can implement all that Jesus is saying to you in these verses. Then pray for the blessing of God on your life as you sink deeper into Him.

Dear Jesus, I want Your blessing on my life.
Show me how to abide in You. In Jesus' name, amen.

CONSOLATION AMID CONFLICT

Our bodies had no rest, but we were troubled on every side.
Outside were conflicts, inside were fears. Nevertheless God, who
comforts the downcast, comforted us by the coming of Titus.
2 CORINTHIANS 7:5–6 NKJV

Sometimes we feel so beaten down by life, battered by outside circumstances over which we have no control. During these unwelcome storms, fear begins to permeate our inner being. Seeing no way out, we may fall into depression and enter into self-preservation mode by withdrawing into ourselves. But in doing so, we cut ourselves off from those who would give us aid and comfort.

Fortunately, God has other plans. He knows what we need and lovingly provides it. He "comforts the downcast" by sending earthly "angels" to help us. These people of God, Tituses among us, give freely of God's love and fill us with the healing balm of His comfort.

In the midst of distress, we are not to withdraw from God's helping hand but to immerse ourselves in His Word and reach out to others, allowing both to give us love and comfort in our times of need. And then, whole once more, we in turn can be a Titus for another.

Dear God, You know my frame, my circumstances, my outlook, my troubles.
Comfort me in this situation through Your Word and the love of others.
Give me consolation in the midst of this conflict. Amen.

THE LOVE LETTER

This is love: not that we loved God, but that he loved us and sent his Son as an atoning sacrifice for our sins.
1 JOHN 4:10 NIV

In the back of her closet, behind sweaters and boxes of seldom-worn shoes, was a carved wooden box. Every so often, she took out the box and slid off the lid. She sat on the carpeted floor in her bedroom and gently lifted out one sheet of paper after another. Each was wrinkled and stained, creased, and worn smooth with reading. Each was written in the same handwriting: her husband's.

Life was busier now; he didn't often tuck love letters under her pillow before he left for work in the morning or wedge a note between the milk and orange juice in the refrigerator. But his heart had not changed. Rereading his old letters helped her remember.

How would her husband have felt if he poured out his love to his wife in a letter and she was too busy or didn't care enough to read it? The same is true with God. And He hasn't just written us a few letters—He's written an entire book! If we want to show Him how much we love Him and desire to understand His heart, we need to read His words.

The Bible is our love letter from God, the one true Lover of our souls. Read it; wear it out!

Dear God, thank You for loving me so much. Thank You for Your living, breathing, life-giving Word. Help me to crave it as I crave food and drink. Amen.

....

....

....

....

....

....

SELF-EXAMINATION

Let us test and examine our ways, and return to the LORD!
LAMENTATIONS 3:40 ESV

What if you could follow yourself around for the day, carefully examining all that you do? Look at your schedule—your choice of activities, the people you talk to, the things you listen to and watch, the habits being formed, the thoughts you think. Maybe your heart desires intimacy with God, but a real day in your life leaves no time for solitude. God often speaks to us in the stillness and in silent spaces. How will we hear Him if we're never still?

Taking time to reflect, to think, and to examine oneself is a necessary step in moving toward intimacy with God. Before we can turn back to Him, we must repent of the things that moved us away from Him in the first place. As we set aside time for solitude and reflection, the Holy Spirit will gently show us these things if we ask. He will show us the sins we need to confess and give us the grace of repentance. As we experience forgiveness, our fellowship with our heavenly Father is restored.

Lord, help me to still myself before You and be willing to examine my ways. Speak to me through Your Holy Spirit about what is wrong in my life. Give me the gift of repentance and allow me to enjoy the sweetness of Your forgiveness.

PRECIOUS MOMENTS

To whom God willed to make known what is the riches of the glory of this mystery among the Gentiles, which is Christ in you, the hope of glory.
COLOSSIANS 1:27 NASB

Do you ever lose sight of just how much you enjoy the presence of God? It's easy to become preoccupied with life's duties. When you finally find a moment to shut out the voices of the day, you quickly discover how little anything else matters but God. He is your light and your salvation. No one knows the path He's chosen for you quite like He does. He points to the truth and brings about the results He destined for you before the beginning of time.

Imagine—you were a thought, an idea with grand purpose, before He ever breathed life into the first man. Compare that to the things that penetrate your mind and cause you concern. In God's presence, there is little to worry about. The truth—freedom from everything—rests in time with Him. The more you lean into His higher purpose, the less you'll try to work it out on your own.

Why spend that precious time telling God all your worries—things He already knows? Instead, give Him minutes of silence and moments of praise, and allow His wisdom to penetrate your heart and direct everything that concerns you.

Lord, help me to never lose sight of how much I enjoy spending time with You. Help me to take time each day to hear what You have to say. Amen.

GOD'S PURPOSES

Though I walk in the midst of trouble, you preserve my life....
The LORD will fulfill his purpose for me.
PSALM 138:7–8 ESV

It's hard to see that the Lord is fulfilling His purpose in our lives when bad things happen, especially in regard to our relationships. These "bad things" usually happen when we place unreal expectations on our family and friends—expectations of security, peace, contentment, or fulfilled needs.

In Psalm 138 David praised God for guiding him through the rough times in his life. As David looked back, he saw God's goodness to him through the good times as well as the bad. And he realized that God would continue to guide his life in the future as He had in the past.

What can we do when life derails our plans, desires, or expectations? First, remember how God has led us through difficult circumstances in the past. Looking back helps us see how God has fulfilled His purpose for saving us: molding us into the image of Christ. Second, thank Him for His guidance and protection as He brings us through hard times. Third, look forward, knowing that God does not allow anything into our lives that isn't for our good. We can trust Him to do what is best for us.

Dear God, help me not to place expectations on my relationships that only You can fulfill. Help me to remember that You are working Your purpose in my life. Amen.

UNEXPECTED TREASURES

Don't fall in love with money. Be satisfied with what you have.
HEBREWS 13:5 CEV

When Dave asked Jen to marry him, he promised her love, faithfulness, and a lifetime of chocolate. He never said anything about money.

As years passed, Jen became increasingly frustrated with broken appliances, calls from bill collectors, and budgets strained to the ripping point. As her family struggled from paycheck to paycheck, she watched friends living comfortably. Discontent and envy stirred in her innards.

The Bible tells us not to fall in love with money, but that's incredibly hard to do—especially if we don't have enough of it. Money becomes a pseudo-savior, a way to rise above problems and enjoy the good things of life. We lose sight of the immeasurable wealth God *has* provided and become lost in the woods of discontent that border our blessings.

Jen recognized the brewing storm in her soul and stepped back to take inventory of the *needs* God had provided for her family rather than focusing on the *wants*. She knew the Lord was embedding gratefulness in her heart the day she found herself dancing with the ailing washing machine as it mamboed across the floor.

Giver of all good things, quench my insatiable thirst for the comfort money provides. Teach me that my security is in You alone. When I fret about money, remind me that Your beloved Son was born on a bale of hay in a barn. Amen.

CARING FOR THE TEMPLE

Honor God with your body.
1 CORINTHIANS 6:20 NLT

Our bodies are amazing gifts from God. Without any thought or effort on our parts, our hearts beat life-giving blood throughout our veins, providing us with the energy to accomplish the thousands of tasks we do each day. Our brains give the commands; our bodies obey. But these incredible structures aren't maintenance-free. Just as we are to be good stewards of our resources of time and money, we should also be good stewards of our bodies. God's Word calls them temples.

When we are busy meeting the needs of others, we often neglect to care for ourselves. But God wants us to treat our bodies with care and respect. This means exercising regularly, eating good food, getting enough rest. These are simple things, but the dividends are high, for when we treat our bodies right, they treat us right in return.

Father, thank You for the amazing body that You have given me,
for all the things it does that happen without my knowledge. Help me
to care for my body in a way that brings honor and glory to You. Amen.

RECEIVING GOD'S EMBRACE

See what great love the Father has lavished on us, that we should be called children of God! And that is what we are!
1 JOHN 3:1 NIV

Some people are born "huggers." They greet family members or complete strangers in the same way—with a hug. They just can't help themselves. They must lavish love on those around them. They must demonstrate affection. Most of us would agree that the closer the relationship, the more meaningful the hug. Can you imagine receiving an embrace from our heavenly Father, the God of the universe?

God lavished His love on us when He sent Jesus to earth. Jesus' sacrificial death on our behalf paved the way for adoption into God's family by faith. When we receive the gift of Jesus, we become children of God. We are no longer strangers. We are no longer alienated from a holy God. We have become family!

As you ponder God's great love for you, picture Jesus hanging on the cross. With arms outstretched, He not only came to embrace the world with God's love—He came to embrace you! Will you receive God's hug? The unconditional love of our Creator is the greatest gift we could ever receive. Will you allow His love to be lavished upon you? Receive the embrace of your heavenly Father today!

Dear Lord, I need Your embrace. May I receive the abundant love You desire to lavish upon me because I am Your child. Amen.

MORE THAN A BEAUTY QUEEN

"If you persist in staying silent at a time like this, help and deliverance will arrive for the Jews from someplace else; but you and your family will be wiped out. Who knows? Maybe you were made queen for just such a time as this."
ESTHER 4:14 MSG

Queens usually begin their lives in royal palaces, living in the lap of luxury.

If someone had told Hadassah, Mordecai's orphaned cousin, that she would become Queen Esther of Persia, she would have laughed in his face! But God had big plans for the lovely Jewish girl. She won an empire-wide beauty contest and King Xerxes's love.

At this point, most fairy tales end with "they lived happily ever after." But even a queen had no guarantee of protection from powerful enemies. Mordecai discovered that Haman, the king's closest advisor, had engineered the genocide of the Jews scattered throughout the empire. While he longed to protect Esther, whom he regarded as his daughter, Mordecai realized that Esther might play a role in saving her people—if she agreed to take the risk.

Few of us live the exotic, thrilling life of a queen, but all women possess power within their spheres of influence—home, work, school, community. God has brought us to this place in history for a purpose. Will we take the risk?

Father, I cannot imagine the plans You have for me.
But I know I can trust You with my hopes, dreams—and life. Amen.

HE IS HERE

And Jacob awaked out of his sleep, and he said,
Surely the LORD is in this place; and I knew it not.
GENESIS 28:16 KJV

No matter where we are, no matter what we are going through, God is with us. Whether we are on the run or rooted in the mud, in conflict with our husband or reaching a compromise, deep in dreams or fully awake, He is here. He is in this place.

Jacob discovered this when he awoke from a dream of angels ascending and descending on a ladder. Having just stolen his brother's blessing, Jacob was on the run. But he could not outrun God. He was still with him, reassuring him, "Behold, I am with you and will keep you wherever you go. . .I will not leave you" (Genesis 28:15 NKJV).

Jacob's God is our God. He has been, is, and always will be with His people. He is the Rock that never moves.

God holds us by the hand, telling us not to be afraid. Through thick and thin, amid dreams and waking hours, while at home and at work, amid laughter and tears, He leads, loves, speaks to, and cares for us. He is here.

Call to Him. He is listening. Love Him. He adores you. Pray to and praise Him. He wants to hear your voice. Reach out and grab His hand. He wants to touch you. Never ever let Him go.

Dear God, my heart overflows with joy and peace in Your presence.
You are here—hallelujah! Your Spirit is with me wherever I go,
whatever I am going through. Thank You, Lord, for never leaving me.

....

....

....

....

....

....

DEEP ROOTS

And he said to the vinedresser, "Look, for three years now I have come seeking fruit on this fig tree, and I find none. Cut it down. . . ." And [the vinedresser] answered him, "Sir, let it alone this year also, until I dig around it and put on manure. Then if it should bear fruit next year, well and good; but if not, you can cut it down."
LUKE 13:7–9 ESV

As we read this parable, we may ask ourselves, Why did God call us to Himself? After all, we often think we'll never win any awards for fruit-bearing. Our marriages often seem fairly ordinary, our testimonies less than exciting, our ministries faithful but limited.

Yet in the same way God did not chop down the barren tree, He has not cut us down. Looking to the future, He digs at our comfortable roots, challenging us to change. Then He fertilizes us with His Word, causing our roots to go deep into faith's soil.

Because God hasn't finished with us yet, let's put ourselves in the path of growth through study, prayer, and fellowship. One day, we'll see that long-awaited fruit and rejoice with God at what He's done through us.

Are we ready to grow? Let's put our roots deep into His Word today.

Lord, thank You for Your gracious love that builds me up instead of cutting me off at the roots. Help my roots go deep in faith today.

A REQUEST FOR WISDOM

Now, O Lord my God, you have made me king instead of my father, David,
but I am like a little child who doesn't know his way around.

1 Kings 3:7 NLT

This prayer occurs one evening after Solomon has replaced David as the king of Israel. God appears to Solomon in a dream and offers to give him whatever he wants. Instead of asking for wealth or long life or triumph over his enemies, Solomon asks for wisdom. Solomon wants to rule wisely but, as he says, he feels like a little child. Therefore, Solomon asks for the ability to decide between right and wrong and to lead his people as a true follower of God.

Solomon's example stands out for us today. We need wisdom in our relationships, particularly as we strive to grow in godliness and love with our spouses.

At some point in your life, perhaps you have felt like a little child. A new situation arises—an argument you've never had before, a life-altering change, the death of a loved one. God is waiting for your prayer, and He desires to guide you in His unsurpassed wisdom. Like little children, we must ask God for help; He will help us find our way.

Dear Lord, You are wise beyond understanding. Grant me Your
wisdom today in my relationships and in my current situations.
Thank You for Your love and guidance. Amen.

BUT SEEK FIRST

But seek ye first the kingdom of God, and his righteousness;
and all these things shall be added unto you.
MATTHEW 6:33 KJV

Times were tough. Her husband's business was slowing down. Bills were beginning to mount. She was torn. Should she seek full-time employment or continue in volunteer ministry? Prayerfully, she and her husband sought the Lord's wisdom. They sensed the Lord asking them to trust Him financially while she served in ministry. By faith they followed the Lord's leading. Soon afterward, an unexpected check came in the mail to cover current expenses. Gradually, her husband's business began to prosper. God supplied their needs as they sought and followed His will.

Many times we are called to make difficult choices. We must glean God's wisdom for discernment. After seeking His wisdom, we must trust Him in obedience. That may require following our heads rather than our hearts or exercising faith rather than succumbing to fear. When we trust and obey, the Lord will take care of the rest. He will reward our faith. He will confirm that His way is indeed the best. He will meet our needs as we follow His will—despite the difficulties. Seek His kingdom and watch the Lord provide for you!

Dear Lord, may I seek You above all else
and trust that You will meet my needs. Amen.

LIFESAVING 101

Examine yourselves as to whether you are in the faith. Test yourselves.
Do you not know yourselves, that Jesus Christ is in you?
2 CORINTHIANS 13:5 NKJV

How many times do we almost drown in the floodwaters of fear? How often are we overcome by waves of discontent or pulled by currents of doubt? How often do we forget that Jesus Christ, the Master of the Universe, is within us? He has already saved us from doubt, disappointment, dread, and death. In His strength, we can move mountains. We can change the world. We can be His representatives of peace, strength, and love within our families, our neighborhoods, and our workplaces.

Jesus, the One with the power to rebuke the winds and calm the waters, is our lifesaver. The knowledge that He is within us boosts us up above the waves of fear and into the peace of His presence.

When caught up in the riptides of life, we are to examine ourselves to make sure we are acknowledging the *fact* that *Christ resides within us*. Buoyed by His presence, we can withstand the storm and rise up in the power of His strength.

Jesus, You are the One who has saved my life, the One who resides within me. Give me the wisdom to keep this in my mind throughout my day, and give me the power to do Your will in this world, knowing You have overcome it. Amen.

DEADLY POISON

Thou shalt not go up and down as a talebearer among thy people:
neither shalt thou stand against the blood of thy neighbour; I am the LORD.
LEVITICUS 19:16 KJV

Gossip is the favorite pastime of far too many Christian women. Probably all of us have been guilty of it at one time or another. The truth is that God hates gossip, and it doesn't matter if a person is a casual talebearer or a chronic one. God is not fooled when we attempt to disguise gossip as prayerful concern, and most people probably aren't fooled either.

The really sad thing is that when we gossip, we often focus our discussion on those we love—our husbands, close friends, or other family members. It's possible that this is because we know more about these people and are more likely to pick up on their faults. Still, it is not right. Gossip is often as deadly as murder.

Another area we fail to acknowledge as gossip is "discussion" with our husbands. It's true that our communication with our spouses should be more open than it is with other people. There are times when talking things over with our husbands is necessary, even though the same conversation with someone else would be gossip. Just be careful not to "overdiscuss" something. Otherwise it begins to fester and boils into talebearing.

Remember: you will not please God if you are prone to gossip.

Oh Lord, I can bring all things before You.
I don't need to spread gossip like a virus.

LOOKING AHEAD TO WHERE GOD IS

*But Jesus told him, "Anyone who puts a hand to the plow
and then looks back is not fit for the Kingdom of God."*
LUKE 9:62 NLT

We know that we shouldn't worry about tomorrow, but even worse is to worry and feel regret about the past, which can only cripple us for tomorrow. "I wish things could be the way they were." "I wish I were younger." "I wish my husband treated me like he did when we first met." "I wish I could fit into those jeans again. . ." I wish, I wish, I wish.

Although the Lord doesn't want us looking back at what once was, our enemy does. He wants us to feel discouraged and helpless over what we face today and drown in self-pity about how it was in the past. But God wants us to look ahead to the future. The future is where He is. He promises to give us hope in our futures. Let's claim that promise for ourselves, for our spouses, and for our marriages. Let's forget the past—it's long gone already and cannot be changed. Let's move ahead and press toward the new things that the Lord wants to do in our lives.

Jesus, please help me to lay aside my past regrets and longings for the things that have already faded away. Let me find contentment in the present and hope for the future. Guide me into the future in accordance with Your will. Amen.

CHANGE

Jesus Christ is the same yesterday and today and forever.
HEBREWS 13:8 NIV

Are you experiencing a lot of change in your life right now? Maybe a career change, a big move, or a child going off to college? Or maybe you aren't facing a huge change, but every day seems to hold quite a few variations and challenges.

Change can be very unsettling and downright scary sometimes. Even the small daily changes tend to eat away at us and have us wishing for something predictable! If we aren't grounded in Christ, change can send us tumbling over the edge. Isn't it wonderful that He gives us the assurance that He will never change? He is the same yesterday, today, and forever! Jesus Christ is with you always. He sees all of the unpredictable moments that creep—or slam—into your life. Remember that these moments have passed through His hands before He allows them to greet you.

Change can actually be a good thing! It might not seem like it at the time, but the Lord will work all things together for your good (Romans 8:28) if you love Him. You can trust that God has a plan for your life and that He will be with you through all of the changes you will face.

Dear Jesus, help me to trust in You through all of the changes in my life. Thank You for never changing and always being there for me. In Your name, amen.

GIANT KILLERS

Go. . . . And may the Lord be with you!
1 Samuel 17:37 NLT

Feeling bullied? Are others trying to fit you into their mold? Are giant-sized problems looming before you?

Welcome to David's world. When he boldly claimed that he would fight Goliath, his brother Eliab assaulted him with dispiriting remarks. But David simply defended his position and then walked away.

King Saul told David he was no match for Goliath. But David, remembering how God had helped him in the past, responded, "The Lord who rescued me from the claws of the lion and the bear will rescue me from this Philistine!" (1 Samuel 17:37 NLT).

The resigned Saul then tried to fit David into his battle gear—an uncomfortable fit for a shepherd boy. So David shed the armor, along with Saul's sword, and picked up his usual weapons—a sling and some stones.

When the Philistine giant saw David, he mocked and abused him. David said, "I come to you in the name of the Lord. . . . Today the Lord will conquer you" (1 Samuel 17:45–46 NLT). Then he took out a stone and hurled it at Goliath. The stone sank into the giant's forehead, and the behemoth fell facedown.

Ladies, we—like David—can refuse to allow the words of discouragers, naysayers, molders, and giants to affect us. We, too, can walk forward in God's name and power. He will help us vanquish every negative word, thought, and deed—and lead us to triumph!

God, give me the strength and the power to walk forth in Your name, to turn away from the negative remarks of others, to be who You've called me to be, and to conquer the giants of this world.

SMART, BRAVE, AND BEAUTIFUL

And it was so, when the king saw Esther the queen standing in the court,
that she obtained favour in his sight: and the king
held out to Esther the golden sceptre.
ESTHER 5:2 KJV

Queen Esther, a lovely Jewish girl who married King Xerxes of Persia, found herself in desperate straits. Not knowing her ethnic background, Haman, her husband's advisor, plotted the annihilation of all Jews throughout the empire. Esther wanted to save her people, but the king had not invited her to his side for thirty days. Had he found a new trophy wife?

Nevertheless, Esther risked her life to connect with Xerxes. She fasted for three days, but Esther did not use a "spiritual" approach in dealing with her husband. Instead, she appeared in royal robes, looking her best. She did not blurt out demands, but piqued the king's curiosity with dinner invitations that included Haman.

By the time Esther presented her request for mercy, Xerxes had offered her half his kingdom. Upon hearing of Haman's treachery, he dispatched him in no time flat.

Few of us win Miss America titles or compete with Martha Stewart's entertainment skills, yet God has gifted us with wisdom, beauty, and hospitality that impact our husbands and others. While we may not rescue an entire nation, we can make a difference in—and even help save—the lives of those around us.

Lord, please help me recognize the gifts You have entrusted
to me and how I can best use them to help others. Amen.

WELL-WATERED GARDENS

*The LORD will guide you always; he will satisfy your needs in
a sun-scorched land.... You will be like a well-watered garden.*
ISAIAH 58:11 NIV

Well-kept gardens are beautiful. The rows of plants are weed-free, the vegetables
and flowers are abundant, and everyone who sees such a garden admires it and
wants the same.

When God is allowed to be our guide, our lives and marriages become like
well-watered gardens. Even in the driest of times, God's beauty can shine through
us. All we have to do is to allow Him the leadership in our homes.

We do this by giving the reins to our husbands. This may sound easy, but often
we want to take control. We want to be a subtle guide, ignoring God's blueprint and
giving our husbands suggestions or bold statements as to how we should be living
as married couples.

This is not God's design and will lead to a garden full of weeds and haphazard
rows. The fruit will be withered, the flowers stunted. If we want a garden that is a
showcase, then we need to step back and let our husbands lead. Even if they don't
seem to be following God's path as we see it, we must trust God to bring His will to
pass. He is a wonderful guide.

*Thank You, Lord, for Your guidance in my life. Help me to
trust You in all things. Help me to believe Your Word. Amen.*

FIRST LABORS

She is energetic and strong, a hard worker.
PROVERBS 31:17 NLT

No matter what our occupations, whether that of homemaker or career woman, God's Word urges women to be hard workers, leading productive lives, not unlike the amazingly fruitful yet nameless wife of noble character described in Proverbs 31:10–31.

Several examples of industrious women can be found in the Bible. In the Old Testament, we can read about Deborah, who was a leader, judge, and prophet. Then there was the widow Ruth, who was faithful to her mother-in-law and who worked in the fields, gathering wheat and barley. In the New Testament is Lydia, who was a dealer in purple cloth. There was also Dorcas, who made clothes. And there was Priscilla, who, along with her tentmaking husband, Aquila, worked in ministry with the apostle Paul. All these women were strong, hard workers.

But our work—whether inside or outside of the home—should not come before our relationships with God or our husbands. In all things, faith and family must come before the deadlines we need to meet, the business trips we need to take, or the garages that need to be cleaned out. Faith and family are even more important than whatever church project we've agreed to direct or community charity drive we've volunteered to participate in.

So let's be good stewards of the time we have here on earth. Give the first and best of your effort, energy, and strength to God and your husband. And the Lord will bless all your labors.

Father, remind me that my first labors are to You and my husband.
Help me to be a good steward of my strength, time, and energy. Amen.

THE SECRET TO CONTENTMENT

I have learned the secret of being content in any and every situation,
whether well fed or hungry, whether living in plenty or in want.
PHILIPPIANS 4:12 NIV

We plan and dream. We imagine a life called *us*. And on the wings of our hopes we see "happily ever after" just over the horizon. The days come and go and dreams give birth to other dreams, until our very happiness is put on a shelf, just out of reach. We wait for the day when our children are a little older or our husbands' work schedules change.

But waiting for the right circumstances to make us happy brings a tension all its own. Very often we mistake this tension as a sign that we are lacking something, but it is actually a tension born out of wanting what we do not have. Contentment, after all, is an inside job, and no amount of rearranging our lives will bring it to us. We must find it within ourselves.

The secret to contentment comes from understanding that where we are now is exactly where God wants us to be. He has a purpose for our lives, and He offers a peace that is separate from our circumstances. When we open our hearts to this truth, love comes rushing in the way the tide fills even the tiniest holes in the sand and blessings are scattered around like seashells.

Lord, help me grow in the holy habit of contentment by
seeking Your presence and purpose for my life. Amen.

DO THE NEXT THING

*"My food," said Jesus, "is to do the will of
him who sent me and to finish his work."*
JOHN 4:34 NIV

Busyness is the curse of modern life. There are lawns to mow, meals to cook, gutters
to clean, gardens to weed—enough chores to last a lifetime of evenings and weekends. Even if you live in a tiny apartment and eat only take-out food, there are still
phone calls to make, floors to scrub, letters to write, and errands to run.

But the Bible says that God has numbered our days as He numbers the hairs on
our heads. He knows how long we have to live, and He knows best what we should
do with the time He has given us.

Christian author and former missionary Elisabeth Elliot gives this advice about
how to decide what to do amid a myriad of necessary and useful things: "Just do the
next thing." These simple words are an echo of Jesus', and in this He is our model.
He did nothing that wasn't God's perfect will, and He was perfectly content. When
we feel harried and stressed, it is often because we are trying to do more than God
has asked us to do.

God always gives us enough time to do His will.

*Dear Father, help me see all the things I have to do and want to do,
and help me order them according to Your will. Amen.*

IN THE ARMS OF A FRIEND

But we all, with unveiled face, beholding as in a mirror the glory
of the Lord, are being transformed into the same image
from glory to glory, just as by the Spirit of the Lord.
2 CORINTHIANS 3:18 NKJV

Shanna found the weeks following the birth of her second son emotional and a true test of faith. Finally, God had proven faithful and restored her newborn to health in spite of the doctor's words: "He only has a fifty-fifty chance of survival." Yet he completely recovered and was home.

The crisis over, Shanna's emotions were more than she could handle, and she found herself at the front door of her friend Barbie. As the door opened, Shanna fell into Barbie's arms.

Fighting to gain her composure, Barbie spoke the words Shanna needed to hear. "It's over. The baby's fine. Now get ahold of your emotions, girl! You're a woman of faith! With God at your side—you won!"

Tears turned to laughter. "I know," Shanna said, "but I needed to hear what you just said."

Have you ever found comfort from God through a friend? God brings His comfort to our hearts in many ways, but often He touches us most through the compassion of our brothers and sisters in Christ. Perhaps God wants to use you to touch someone today. Are you willing?

Thank You, Lord, for friendships. Give me compassion and
a willingness to be used as Your hand in someone's life. Amen.

....

....

....

....

....

....

THE RIVER

Consider it pure joy. . .whenever you face trials of many kinds.
JAMES 1:2 NIV

Finding joy in the trials of life is like finding a precious stone embedded along a river's edge. As the water rages on, it is almost impossible to spot the stone's vibrant colors, but when the water is still, it is easy to see how it has been there all along. These are deep lessons that, when gathered together, strengthen our faith.

Turning away from trials is our natural response to life, but if we remember the river and the treasures that await us, they become easier to bear. Jesus tells us that throughout life we will have many troubles. At the same time, He offers us strength by reminding us that He has overcome them all (John 16:33). This is of great comfort to us when life becomes the raging river and we are struggling just to keep our heads above the water.

In time, as the water of our days ebbs and flows, eventually the turbulence passes. We gasp and cough and cling to shore to find that we survived not only the current that threatened to pull us under, but our own doubts as well. And blinking to us in the sunlight, caught along the riverbank, are pearls of wisdom and a jewel called hope.

Father, I fear the trials when they come, but I know that You are always with me. Help me cling to You when troubles come, believing that through faith there is a lesson waiting for me in the end. Amen.

TREASURES OF LOVE

*He chose us in Him before the foundation of the world, that we would be holy
and blameless before Him. In love He predestined us to adoption as sons
through Jesus Christ to Himself, according to the kind intention of His will.*

EPHESIANS 1:4–5 NASB

God sees us the way we seldom see ourselves—holy, pure, and blameless. It seems impossible. Did He forget the day we impatiently shifted back and forth in line, sending mental daggers to the person ahead, who moved too slowly? Or all the times we complain and fret when our plans do not unfold in the way we hope?

We start our day with good intentions. But in our rush to achieve and be, we aim, fall short, and miss the mark, not seeing that who we are has already been named. We have already been claimed. And because of Christ's loving sacrifice, we are free to see ourselves as we really are—chosen and beloved.

Picked out of the refuse of our failures, we are restored and covered in a blanket of His grace. Set apart for a glorious purpose, we are bestowed with the jewels of His love. It is not He who forgets, but rather we who need to remember. We are His living treasure here on earth.

Like the way light pours through a diamond, His light reflects best through the love we offer to others, especially to our husbands. We are not to be hidden away for safekeeping, for only in use do the jewels of compassion, kindness, gentleness, and patience (Colossians 3:12) sparkle brightly against a dark and colorless world.

*Father, help me to reflect Your love through my words and
deeds so that when others see me, they really see You. Amen.*

IN GOD'S PRESENCE

Glory and honour are in his presence;
strength and gladness are in his place.
1 CHRONICLES 16:27 KJV

It is impossible for us with our imperfect minds to grasp the greatness of God. It is simply beyond our comprehension. However, God's Word gives us some really amazing insight into His character.

You know, in the Old Testament very few people were allowed into God's presence in the Holy of Holies because God is just that—holy. Now, because of Christ's blood, that veil separating the Holy Place from the Holy of Holies has been torn in two. Jesus is our High Priest, and because of that we have access to the Father. This doesn't make God less holy. It just means that because of Christ's blood those barriers have been removed.

In God's presence are glory, honor, strength, gladness, and a host of other wonderful characteristics. Our God is truly awesome. We can see that in creation, at Calvary, at the garden tomb, and in our own lives.

Yes, God wants very much to be involved in our lives. He wants to be included in every aspect of our marriages, families, careers, and so forth. Great God that He is, He still cares for each of us individually. How about it? Will *you* let Him have the primary place in your home?

It's hard to understand why a great God like You would want to invest
so much in a sinner like me, but I'm so thankful that You do, Lord.

BEAUTY IS FLEETING

Charm is deceptive, and beauty is fleeting;
but a woman who fears the Lord is to be praised.
PROVERBS 31:30 NIV

Let's face it. The aging process begins the moment we take our first breath. It's undeniable. We may color our gray or undergo plastic surgery, but we will never again look as we did in our twenties—something society tries to convince us is a problem. Accept the fact that beauty is fleeting. Years of gravitational pull eventually take their toll. Our physical bodies were not created to live forever. Someday we will return to the dust from which we were made.

Do not be distraught. Be encouraged! The Lord reminds us that the spiritual aspect of the aging process is far more important than our physical bodies. Our physical lives are for a season. Our spiritual lives are forever!

Choose to age gracefully by concentrating on the spiritual aspect of your being. Live in awe and respect for the Lord. Realize that your relationship with Him is the most important thing in this life. Then you will be able to laugh at your wrinkles while embracing your grandchildren. Your inner beauty will shine forth by the transforming power of the Holy Spirit. You will truly become more beautiful with each passing day!

Dear Lord, my physical beauty may not last forever, but my
relationship with You will. So help me focus on that! Amen.

GOD'S WONDER WOMAN

Now Deborah, a prophetess, the wife of Lapidoth,
was judging Israel at that time.
JUDGES 4:4 NKJV

Prophet. Judge. Wife. Mother. All these describe Deborah, a remarkable woman who answered God's leadership call and governed Israel for sixty years. In an era when women did not learn to read, let alone interpret the Law, Deborah held court every day under a palm tree. Her countrymen arrived from near and far to entrust their disputes to Deborah's godly insights. We don't know Lapidoth's reaction, but during Old Testament times, a woman could not act without her husband's consent. So by God's grace, Deborah managed her home at the same time she managed the nation.

During the early years of Deborah's tenure, Israel struggled with unstable spiritual and political conditions. Many worshipped idols; as a result, God could not bless them. For twenty years, Jabin, the cruel Canaanite king, and his general, Sisera, made constant raids on their villages. Then God spoke through Deborah, summoning Barak to lead an army against Sisera's forces. Barak refused to go to war without Deborah, so she traveled far from home to experience the same dangers he and his soldiers faced. God led them to victory and disposed of Sisera through Jael, another woman. Deborah's praise welled up in a warlike song of triumph that reminded the Israelites to worship their powerful, wonderful God.

God has equipped each of us with the ability to perform the duties to which He has called us. Are you letting Him work His way in your life?

Father, I often limit the possibilities You envision for me.
Help me to dream Your dreams. Amen.

BURDEN BEARING

The heartfelt counsel of a friend is as sweet as perfume and incense.
PROVERBS 27:9 NLT

Janet's friends and family often came to her for advice. She always seemed to have just the right words to say. Lately, though, she was feeling overwhelmed because it seemed like everyone needed her at once. Besides, she had her own problems and responsibilities. What she really wanted was some time away—from her loved ones *and* their problems.

Caring for others, listening to them, and offering wise counsel is biblical. God created us to live in community, and we are instructed to bear one another's burdens. But there is often a fine line between bearing others' burdens and bearing *responsibility* for their burdens. It drains us and, more importantly, can keep them from seeking answers directly from God.

It's essential to remember that our job is to point others *to* Christ, not become a substitute for Him. Allowing our friends unlimited access to our advice and counsel is one way this can happen. Sometimes the wisest words of advice we can offer are "tell it to Jesus."

Father, help me to wisely discern the difference between bearing others' burdens and taking responsibility for their problems. Help me to point others to You. Amen.

FAITH BOOSTER

Therefore by Him let us continually offer the sacrifice of praise to God,
that is, the fruit of our lips, giving thanks to His name.
HEBREWS 13:15 NKJV

Don't we just love it when people say "thank you" after we've done something for them? For some reason, it makes us more willing to perform some other duty, maybe an even greater task than the one we've already provided.

On the flip side, we consider it somewhat rude, even a bit disheartening, when we don't get that simple "thank you" for our efforts—whether that person is our spouse, our child, a neighbor, or a stranger on the street.

Imagine God not getting a thank-you for all He's done for us. Imagine His disappointment when we neglect to say those two simple words.

Remember when Jesus healed the ten lepers and only one, a Samaritan, "returned, and with a loud voice glorified God, and fell down on his face at His feet, giving Him thanks" (Luke 17:15–16 NKJV)? What was Jesus' response? "But where are the nine? Were there not any found who returned to give glory to God except this foreigner?" (Luke 17:17–18 NKJV).

Be like that good Samaritan: "Consider what great things [the Lord] has done for you" (1 Samuel 12:24 NKJV) and give Him thanks. When you do, you will be not only pleasing God but also boosting your faith as you remember all the ways He has answered your prayers in the past. Such assurance of His hand in your life cannot help but fill you with peace.

So go ahead—make God's day. Thank Him, and then bask in that peace that surpasses all understanding (Philippians 4:6–7 NKJV).

Dear God, there are so many things You have done for me.
So here I am, falling down at Your feet to shout, THANK YOU!

CASTING AWAY ANXIETY

Therefore humble yourselves under the mighty hand of God, that He may exalt you in due time, casting all your care upon Him, for He cares for you.
1 PETER 5:6–7 NKJV

A young bride stands at the window late at night, willing her husband's return from working late. He hasn't called to tell her where he is or what time to expect him home. Any moment now, she's sure the police will be at her door to tell her she's a widow.

Parents sit at the bedside of their child who is sick, unable to comprehend the illness that is sucking the life from her. Or a husband loses his job and is unable to find another quickly. The bills are piling up because there is no money to pay them.

These are extreme examples of circumstances that cause us to be anxious. Yet the little things cause just as much worry as the big things. The Amplified Bible expands on the word *care* in 1 Peter 5:7 by lumping together all our anxieties, all our worries, and all our concerns.

With every anxiety, God calls us to throw everything on Him, to let go of the burden of worry, large or small. The picture here is one of Him gathering them all together into one sack and carrying it on His shoulders. He wants to be our burden-bearer because He is able, because He cares for us affectionately and watchfully.

He knows the burden of anxiety we carry. Roll it off onto His mighty shoulders today.

Father, give me the strength to let go of this burden of anxiety I carry.
You desire to bear my burden for me because of Your awesome love.
Thank You for carrying my load. Amen.

PLEASING GOD OR PLEASING SELF

Obviously, I'm not trying to win the approval of people, but of God.
If pleasing people were my goal, I would not be Christ's servant.
GALATIANS 1:10 NLT

A Christian camp director read the following statement, burning it into the minds of his listeners: "Only two choices on the shelf, pleasing God or pleasing self."

While this statement should sum up all our relationships, it especially applies in marriage. There is no room for selfishness in a marriage.

In Galatians 1:10 Paul states that his goal is to please God. And the proof he gives is that he wouldn't be serving Christ as he did if he were seeking to please others or himself. He could have done without the aggravations, the misunderstandings, and the persecutions he experienced. Yet he accepted them because *he* no longer mattered—only by choosing to please God instead of others or himself was he fulfilled and content.

Most of us wives fall into the trap of people-pleasing. But it seems that the harder we try to please others, the less we are fulfilled.

When we choose to put our focus on pleasing God, it doesn't matter what people say about us. Only in pleasing God, being obedient to His commands and guidelines for life, especially in our marriage relationships, do we truly feel fulfilled and content.

Father, I long to hear the words, "Well done, My good and faithful servant."
Help me choose to please You in all things today, for only then am I satisfied. Amen.

THE BIBLE IN A NUTSHELL

The next day John saw Jesus coming toward him and said,
"Look, the Lamb of God, who takes away the sin of the world!"
JOHN 1:29 NIV

These words of John, spoken soon after Jesus' baptism in the Jordan River, contain the essence of the Bible in a nutshell. Though the Bible was written by different men from different countries, in different languages, over a span of thousands of years, it has a singular focus: Jesus. The books of history, law, and prophecy in the Old Testament point ahead to Jesus' coming; the Gospels and epistles of the New Testament point back to His ministry on earth and ahead to His heavenly reign. Essentially, the Bible is like a big neon arrow shining in the darkness, pointing to Jesus, saying as John did, "Look, the Lamb of God!"

The Bible may be our road map to heaven, but if we don't read it, we may lose the way. The world flashes many bright and enticing things before our eyes. Detours, shortcuts, potholes, and pitfalls in the form of missed opportunities, wrong choices, and sinful relationships all threaten to derail our spiritual journey.

The world will try to pull our eyes away from Jesus. Staying faithful to reading and meditating on God's Word will keep our eyes focused where they should be, on the Author and Perfecter of our faith (Hebrews 12:2).

Dear Father, Your Word is a lamp to my feet and a light to my path.
Help me read Your Word daily and keep my eyes fixed on Jesus. Amen.

FLYING OFF THE HANDLE

A gentle response defuses anger,
but a sharp tongue kindles a temper-fire.
PROVERBS 15:1 MSG

The "love is patient, love is kind" passage in Paul's letter to the Corinthians (1 Corinthians 13:4 NIV) is one of the world's most well-known descriptions of love. After giving the positive attributes of love, Paul flips the coin to explain what love is *not*: it is not rude or easily angered.

The Greek word for "easily angered" is *paroxynō*. In different Bible versions, it is translated to mean greatly distressed, easily angered, irritable. Bottom line, Paul was saying that love means we don't fly off the handle with our husbands and children.

When we snap at those we love, what happens? Our actions create emotional and physical distance. People scatter! They escape to another room until we cool off. Or they might respond by getting even and snapping back. Irritability can quickly escalate into anger. Little things turn into big things, and big things turn into bad things.

We all have frustrating days that put us close to the edge. So what's a better way to handle irritability? Instead of expecting your family to excuse bad behavior after it happens, ask for some allowance. Be candid—before you snap. "I've had a horrible day and I'm not feeling very patient" is a much healthier response than flying off the handle.

Try it! There's nothing to lose and everything to gain: real love.

Lord, put a bit in my mouth! Pull on the reins so that I stop before I snap.

SHEEP AND SHEPHERD

I will be like a shepherd looking for his scattered flock.
I will find my sheep and rescue them from all the places
where they were scattered on that dark and cloudy day.
EZEKIEL 34:12 NLT

We've probably read passages about shepherds and their flocks before now. Throughout the Bible, shepherd imagery is prevalent. In many cases, the shepherd leads his flock and the sheep follow him trustingly. In Ezekiel, God describes Himself as a shepherd looking for his lost flock. The sheep to which God refers are not following their Shepherd in a nice straight line, but rather, they are scattered. Whether driven away by fear of the weather or having simply wandered off through inattention, these sheep have ended up in dangerous places from which the Shepherd must rescue them.

This image of God as our Shepherd is a wonderful complement to the image of the shepherd leading his flock. This image assures us that if we somehow get distracted by carelessness or fear, God will come looking for us. We are not completely lost and abandoned if we somehow wander away. Even when we find ourselves in dangerous places, we can have the confidence that our Shepherd will rescue us from all danger, bringing us back to the fold and eventually leading us to good pastures and to rest.

Dear Lord, thank You for being my Shepherd. Thank You for not only
leading me in safe paths but also rescuing me when I go astray.
I'm so thankful You care so much about me. Amen.

ANXIETY AND GOD-WORSHIP

If you decide for God, living a life of God-worship,
it follows that you don't fuss about what's on the table at
mealtimes or whether the clothes in your closet are in fashion.
MATTHEW 6:25 MSG

Jesus knows how to get to the heart of any problem. In the Sermon on the Mount He touched on a number of topics, but He especially focused on things that cause anxiety. He said that the cure for anxiety is deciding to live a life of God-worship. When our thoughts are totally focused on God, we won't fuss about what we're going to eat or whether we're dressed in the latest fashions.

As women, we tend to worry about the everyday necessities of life. And it's easy to blame our husbands when these needs are jeopardized. Food and clothing are basic needs, but at times it seems that women are more concerned with these issues than men, probably because of our nurturing natures. We need to be careful that we don't put more emphasis on the necessities than God does.

If we decide for God, we must trust that He will provide exactly what we need. While it may not be gourmet food or haute couture, we can be content, knowing that many times He gives us our wants as well. Trust God to provide; rest in His love. And thank Him for every provision. God loves to receive our worship for what we take for granted.

Father, thank You for providing all that we need,
many times even more than we ask for. You are good. Amen.

LIGHT FOR A DARK JOURNEY

And I will bring the blind by a way that they knew not; I will lead them in paths that they have not known: I will make darkness light before them, and crooked things straight. These things will I do unto them, and not forsake them.
ISAIAH 42:16 KJV

Blind people depend on unchanging organization in their homes to help them navigate through life. No one can shift a piece of furniture. Every pan or dish must find its given place in a cabinet after washing. Matching clothes must be grouped together, or the blind person may walk out the door wearing a color combination never conceived in the civilized world!

Given such dependence on everyday consistency, why would God take blind people down unfamiliar paths where they might fall? And while most of us possess physical sight, we may often find ourselves in dark circumstances where we feel ignorant, confused, even helpless. Does God enjoy our struggles? Does He laugh when we stumble?

No. Isaiah tells us that God promises to do the impossible for His blind, stressed people: He will give light to those who don't even know what it is. He will straighten our paths in ways we could never envision. Just as a faithful friend guides a blind person through a dangerous intersection in a strange city, God will help us deal with the unknown. He never leaves us alone.

Lord Jesus, my humanity blinds me to Your possibilities.
Please hold my hand and lead me along Your way. Amen.

LIGHT

You, LORD, are my lamp; the LORD turns my darkness into light.
2 SAMUEL 22:29 NIV

The Bible begins with light. Genesis 1:3 tells us, "And God said, 'Let there be light,' and there was light" (NIV). It also ends with light. Revelation 22:5 says, "There will be no more night. They will not need the light of a lamp or the light of the sun, for the Lord God will give them light" (NIV). Unfortunately, there's a lot of darkness in between. War. Murder. Pain. Loss. Scripture certainly doesn't sugarcoat the difficulties of life; however, even in the midst of the darkness there are glorious glimpses of His marvelous light. David's sin is forgiven, and he becomes a man after God's own heart. Paul is transformed from a murderer of Christians to a passionate evangelist. Peter denied Christ, but that wasn't his destiny—instead he defends Christ to the death. God has the amazing ability to turn even our darkest situations into personal and spiritual victories.

Perhaps you are facing a dark situation right now. Maybe you've suffered loss, experienced a moral failure, or missed a chance to defend your faith. If so, you're not alone—you have a lot of company. When it seems that you're surrounded by darkness, remember that light is both your foundation and your future. Release the situation to God's marvelous light and know that He is able to transform it into something more than you could ever dream.

*God, you are Light. In you there is no darkness at all. Thank You
for the truth that Your light illumines even my blackest night.*

THE POWER OF PRAYER

*For the eyes of the Lord are on the righteous and his ears are attentive
to their prayer, but the face of the Lord is against those who do evil.*

1 PETER 3:12 NIV

The Bible tells us that when two or more are gathered together in Jesus' name, He is right there with them (Matthew 18:20)! God's Word also tells us that the prayers of the righteous are "powerful and effective" (James 5:16 NIV). Are you praying with others on a regular basis? If you are living a godly life, your prayers have power, and when two of you are praying together. . .there is even more power!

Most of us lead very busy lives, and we're lucky if we can squeeze in our own private prayer time, let alone find the time to pray with others. But we need to do whatever we can to *make* time to pray with others—whether in person, over the phone, by texting, or via the Internet.

Prayer ushers us into the presence of God. Prayer allows us to hear and echo the needs of others. Prayer changes things. Prayer is crucial to a growing marriage, a burgeoning family, and your very life!

*Father, I come here now, in Your name, to praise You, to know You more,
and to lift my concerns up to You. Help me make prayer a
priority in my marriage, my family, my life. Amen.*

GOD'S PICKET FENCE

The name of the Lord is a strong tower;
the righteous runs into it and is safe.
PROVERBS 18:10 NASB

It's a dangerous world out there. Drunk drivers, heart attacks, rabid dogs, cancer, unemployment, terrorism, E. coli. . . The list goes on. It is easy to use a lot of energy thinking about all the bad things that could happen, as if our mental vigilance will somehow ward them off. But the Bible is very clear in commanding us not to worry. Jesus says it in unmistakably direct language: "Do not worry" (Matthew 6:31 NIV). We should be very wary about disobeying a direct command from Jesus!

At its root, worry shows our lack of trust in both God's love and His power. The Bible is as clear about God's promises of protection for those who love Him as it is about the injunction not to worry. In fact, one necessarily follows the other: we shouldn't worry *because* God is taking care of us. The Bible says that we can rejoice; we can spend our days singing praise to God, knowing that His protection is all around us.

We don't always have fences around our houses, and even if we did, they couldn't protect our families from everything. But what we do have is a promise from God that He stands as an eternal sentry over those who love Him.

Dear Lord, I praise You for Your immense power, Your love, and Your faithfulness.
Forgive me for worrying, and help me trust in Your promises. Amen.

RECEIVING THE UNDESERVED

But the Lord our God is merciful and forgiving,
even though we have rebelled against him.
DANIEL 9:9 NLT

Rebellion is a word one comes across in many different contexts. One reads of historical rebellion, of literary rebellion, even of rebellious teenagers. Regardless of the context, rebellion—the flagrant defiance of the authority in charge—is often seriously punished. Rarely does one come across a case where outright rebellion is treated with mercy and forgiveness.

In his prayer to God, Daniel admits that he and his people have rebelled against God and His word. Punishment is the obvious recompense for such behavior. But Daniel doesn't talk about punishment; he speaks instead about the incredible mercy and forgiveness of God.

As Christians today, we remain a people of unclean hearts, rebellious and disobedient toward God. And yet, despite our rebellion, we serve a God who loves and cares for us, a God who desires reconciliation above all else, a God who sent His Son to die on the cross so that our sins could be washed away once and for all. Instead of punishment, we are graced with God's mercy and forgiveness. Praise God for His infinite love!

Dear Lord, although I sometimes rebel against You, You continually show
me forgiveness and mercy. Thank You for loving me so. Teach me to obey
Your Word today and every day. Help me live to please You. Amen.

THE FIRST AND LAST WORD

*O God, You are my God; early will I seek You.... When I remember You
on my bed, I meditate on You in the night watches. Because You have
been my help, therefore in the shadow of Your wings I will rejoice.
My soul follows close behind You; Your right hand upholds me.*

PSALM 63:1, 6–8 NKJV

Nothing starts a day out better than spending some moments in God's Word. Our perspective shifts, becoming His, not ours. We notice the wonder of His creation, seeing His hand in each leaf of the tree, each feather on the bird, each hair on our husband's head, and, in so doing, we are moved to praise Him for His glorious works.

As the day progresses, we turn to feel Him beside us, surrounding us, supporting us. We occasionally send up desperate prayers and are then strengthened as we feel His reassuring hand upon our shoulder. At times, we hear Him whisper and stop what we're doing to listen. And then, in God's power, we step out of our comfort zone to heed His direction.

When the day is done and we are about to close our eyes, we open His Book to hear the last word of the day. As we focus on the Light, the world fades away, losing its strength, its hold over us, and we are renewed in His wisdom, falling asleep in the quiet comfort of His ever-loving, everlasting arms.

*Lord, be my help, my guide, my strength as I seek the light
of Your Word—day and night.*

A MASTER BUILDER

Every wise woman buildeth her house.
PROVERBS 14:1 KJV

What does your dream home look like? Is it a log cabin in the woods? A mansion in the country? A beachfront condo? Whatever it is, it takes skill to build. And while you may hire a contractor and construction crew to erect the physical structure, you are the actual builder of your home.

The most important part of any building is the foundation, and there is no surer foundation than Christ. He must be at the center of your family life. It is His wisdom that makes a home strong, His love that holds the bricks and mortar together. Once He is established as the groundwork for your structure, you can successfully add the walls, roof, and all of the interior details.

Your home should be a refuge from the world. A place that reflects who you are. It should feel warm and welcoming, tranquil and content. If it doesn't, then perhaps it's time to take a second look at your building materials. Don't settle for less than the best.

Remember that the home you are erecting now will become a heritage for generations to come. Dream big, dream bright, and with the right tools and a sure foundation, that dream will become a reality.

Dear Father, help me to be a wise builder, to make my home a peaceful habitation that will stand the test of time and remain long after I am gone. Amen.

RAISED SCARS

And as we have borne the image of the man of dust,
we shall also bear the image of the heavenly Man.
1 CORINTHIANS 15:49 NKJV

As wives, daughters, mothers, and friends, we all bear scars from painful experiences. Some scars are visible, like the ones from childhood spills or the marks from an appendectomy, cesarean section, or some other surgery. Then there are the scars that are less visible. The wounds on our hearts when our husband speaks a cross word, a loved one has died, or a cherished relationship has been severed.

Yes, we all bear scars. But with Jesus in our hearts, we, although wounded, still have the victory. We have been born anew into the life of Christ. Nothing in this world can ever truly harm us, for the Great Healer lives within. Amid the wounds and suffering of this world, we can access His peace, His life, His power.

Yes, like Jesus after the Resurrection on that long-ago Easter morn, we still bear the scars of this world on our hands, our feet, our sides. They are proof of the pain we have endured. But because our Champion rose again—with His wounds disfiguring but not disabling—we are more than enabled to live mighty lives in Christ.

Don't let the scars you bear disable you. Instead, experience the peace, strength, healing, and victory you have in Christ. Then rise anew in His power!

Dear God, You know my scars inside and out. Although the wounds
have healed, the scars remain. But Your Son has given me power,
victory, and strength over the pain of this world. In Him I have peace.
Thank You for giving us Your Son and raising Him again!

WHO DO YOU RUN TO?

*Immediately, when the entire crowd saw Him,
they were amazed and began running up to greet Him.*
MARK 9:15 NASB

After Jesus' transfiguration, He came down the mountain. As soon as the people saw Him, they ran to greet Him. When Jesus asked what was happening, a man spoke up, telling Jesus how His disciples were having trouble healing his son, a boy who was seized by a mute spirit.

After giving Jesus an update on his boy's condition, the father said, "If You can do anything, take pity on us and help us!" (Mark 9:22 NASB).

Jesus responded with, " 'If You can?' All things are possible to him who believes" (Mark 9:23 NASB).

The boy's father cried out, "I do believe; help my unbelief" (Mark 9:24 NASB).

When the crowd began to gather around, Jesus rebuked the boy's unclean spirit, and he was healed.

What do you do when you're having trouble at home? Who do *you* run to? Are you running to Jesus, pleading for Him to help you? Do you know that if you only believe, *anything* is possible? Are you confirming that belief to Jesus and asking Him for more?

Run to Jesus. Tell Him all. Cry out for more faith. And watch the miracles commence!

*Jesus, I run to You today, amazement in my eyes, my heart in my hand,
my troubles on my shoulders. Help me, Lord! Take pity upon me!
I do believe in You—help my unbelief! Show me a miracle!*

PICTURE WINDOW

But the path of the righteous is like the light of dawn,
which shines brighter and brighter until full day.
PROVERBS 4:18 ESV

Have you ever looked at a classic stained-glass window at night? You don't see much. Though the leading around each form may give an outline of the subject, you can't see the bright colors that make such windows so appealing in the daylight.

When the sun rises, colors begin to appear, and as bright sunlight shines through the panes of glass, a beautiful picture appears, portraying biblical characters or parables—most often Jesus.

Our lives are like those windows. Before we know Jesus, our window is dark. But when we come to know Him, His light shines in us and a spiritual picture appears—faintly, perhaps, at first, but with much potential for brightness. As we grow in Him, His light brightens and our testimonies shine forth with increasing beauty.

Can those around us testify to the light shining through our lives? Do the robes of Jesus shine whitely, or has sin muddied the picture, blocking His light from our witness? As Jesus influences our marriages, our paths shine first in the power of dawn sunshine then ever increasing, till a more-than-noonday brightness enlivens all the colors of our picture window.

Lord, help me to live in Your brightness and reflect that light in my life.
May my husband and others clearly see my testimony of faith.

OFFENSIVE WAYS

Worry. Anxiety. Fear. It is easy to become consumed with anxious thoughts, the "what-ifs" in life. What if my breast lump turns out to be malignant? What if my husband gets laid off? What if my friend doesn't forgive me? Our mind dwells on scenarios that may or may not come to pass. Mental and emotional energy is expended needlessly because worrying changes nothing. Instead, we are the ones adversely affected. The stress generated by worry can cause physical, mental, and emotional illnesses.

Worry, anxiety, and fear are also spiritual roadblocks. Did you know that anxious thoughts are offensive to God? Anxiety is a red flag signaling that we are not trusting God. Fear and faith cannot coexist. We are either worrying or trusting, anxious or peaceful.

Come before the Lord. Invite Him to search your heart. Allow His light to expose any anxious thoughts lurking in the shadows. Acknowledge and confess your fears. Then trust Him with those concerns. Ask that His will be done, knowing and believing that His will is best. Then receive His peace by faith. Desire to live by faith, trusting all your cares to God.

Dear Lord, search my heart. Forgive my anxious thoughts.
May I trust You instead. Amen.

GRACE—IT'S STILL AMAZING

Create in me a clean heart, O God;
and renew a right spirit within me.
PSALM 51:10 KJV

Do you hold grudges? Sometimes it's really hard to let go of grief and anger when someone has caused you hurt and pain. And it's often the ones who know you best that can hurt you the most.

You trusted them, perhaps opened up and became transparent, leaving yourself vulnerable. Maybe you've resolved never to do that again. Holding on to offenses, remembering the incident, and experiencing those feelings over and over again can't hurt the person who hurt you—it only hurts *you*.

The greatest gift you can give yourself is to forgive the offender. It's hard to let go, but think of it not as letting go but as giving it up—giving it to God. Make a trade-off. Give Him your shame, anger, guilt, and memories of the assault or insult. Then when you're empty, really empty, let Him fill you with His grace! Try it, and you'll find that grace is still amazing every single time you experience it.

Lord, help me to let go of the injuries I've experienced at the hands of others,
from the smallest little hurt to the deepest wounds of my heart. Show me
how to really let them go and live in Your grace every day! Amen.

QUEENLY LISTENING

To answer before listening—that is folly and shame.
PROVERBS 18:13 NIV

Nebuchadnezzar's wife, the queen, had been widowed for some time when her grandson, Belshazzar, decided to throw a big banquet. The queen wasn't planning on attending the party, but then she heard voices, upset and frightened. She was told that a hand had mysteriously appeared and written words on the banquet wall.

No one could interpret the meaning of the writing, but the queen knew someone who could. She hurried into the banquet hall to find King Belshazzar. "This man Daniel, whom the king [Nebuchadnezzar] called Belteshazzar, was found to have a keen mind and knowledge and understanding, and also the ability to interpret dreams, explain riddles and solve difficult problems. Call for Daniel, and he will tell you what the writing means" (Daniel 5:12 NIV).

This queen had apparently listened to her husband throughout their marriage—really, really listened. She was raised in a pagan culture and was probably very young when she married King Nebuchadnezzar, yet she had the wisdom to pay attention to her husband's dramatic problems. On this fateful day, the knowledge she had gleaned was used to accomplish God's purposes.

Listening, really listening, is a rare trait. We all need to listen more attentively to our husbands, our children, our friends. We might learn something!

Father, sometimes I talk too much! Teach me to be a good listener to others.
Stop me as I start to interrupt someone so that I can hold back and just listen.

NO PLACE LIKE HOME

She looketh well to the ways of her household,
and eateth not the bread of idleness.
PROVERBS 31:27 KJV

Taking care of a home is a lot of work, and no one can manage yours better than you!

You know where everything is. You know how much food to prepare to feed your family. You know when to start dinner to make sure it's served at the appropriate time. You're the queen of clean, a whiz at obliterating stubborn stains. You're a bargain hunter, getting the most for your money. When something needs doing, you roll up your sleeves and get to work. Your home is your pride and joy, and it shows!

If you have a lovely home, you know that it didn't get that way by chance. It took a lot of effort, and a great deal of that effort came from you. Give yourself a pat on the back. You have created a place of comfort and beauty that blesses your entire family. With your labor and skill, there truly is no place like home!

Dear heavenly Father, thank You for my home and family. Help me
to always cherish it and care for it as You would have me to. Amen.

SPIRITUAL HEALTH TIPS

But ye, beloved, building up yourselves on your most holy faith, praying
in the Holy Ghost, keep yourselves in the love of God, looking for
the mercy of our Lord Jesus Christ unto eternal life.
JUDE 1:20–21 KJV

Women spend untold time and energy nurturing other people—a lifelong commitment to Jesus' command to love our neighbors as ourselves. Sometimes, however, we're so busy working, planning, celebrating, comforting, listening, and chauffeuring that we forget to invest in our own spiritual health.

Jude calls on Christians to exercise their faith so they will not only survive but also thrive in a culture that does not worship God. Of course, exercise is never easy! We may spend days in endless activity, yet our spiritual muscles grow flabby because we never stretch them beyond the status quo. When we dare to dream God's dreams and follow His direction, we gain the power to accomplish His will.

Jude urges believers to connect with the Holy Spirit in fervent lifestyle prayer and remain close to God, not wandering off to embrace destructive values and habits.

Finally, he encourages his friends to remain upbeat on a major scale: "Expect God's mercy through Jesus Christ to bless you forever!"

When we follow God's regimen for good spiritual health, we can anticipate great things in our own lives and in the lives of those we serve.

Lord Jesus, I don't like change—yet if I'm to grow and help others develop,
I need to welcome it! Transform me, God. Amen.

LIFT UP GOD'S NAME

O Lord, thou art my God; I will exalt thee, I will praise thy name; for thou hast done wonderful things; thy counsels of old are faithfulness and truth.

ISAIAH 25:1 KJV

Kendra sat at the kitchen table savoring the last of her coffee and enjoying her morning fellowship with her Savior. The brightness of the sun streaming through the window caught her attention, and she automatically looked toward the east, where the bright orb was just coming over the horizon. She gasped at the scene before her. Bold oranges coupled with rich pink hues and soft blues bathed the country landscape in a flood of cheerful color that only God could have created.

She wondered for perhaps the millionth time how anyone could doubt the existence of this great Creator. Not only did God paint beautiful pictures in His creation; He also was the Master Potter who was in the process of molding her into a vessel fit for His use.

How thankful Kendra was to have God in her life. He who made her knew her best. He would give her the strength and wisdom to do her best in everything—her marriage, her career, her service to Him. He is truly a faithful and awesome God!

How amazing You are, O God. Your hand in creation and Your hand on my life are continual reminders of Your greatness.

POUR OUT YOUR SOUL

But Hannah replied, "No, my lord, I am a woman oppressed
in spirit. . .I have poured out my soul before the LORD."
1 SAMUEL 1:15 NASB

Hannah of the Bible had major problems. She was having trouble conceiving and, because of that, was antagonized by her husband's other wife, the child-bearing Peninnah.

So what did she do? She poured out her soul to God. Then, after leaving all her cares at her Father's feet, she "went her way and ate, and her face was no longer sad" (1 Samuel 1:18). The next day, she and her family rose up early and worshipped the Lord (1 Samuel 1:19). Soon after, she conceived. The Lord had answered her prayer.

Are we as smart as Hannah? Do we go to the Lord when we are distressed and pour out our hearts before Him? Or do we sit and simmer in the juices of discontentment, sucking up our hurts and sorrows, becoming so weighed down by our woes that we have trouble even rising to our feet?

Got trouble? Get talking. Pour out your heart before the Lord. He is ready and waiting to listen. Give Him the desires of your heart. Leave your troubles at His feet. And then, knowing all is in His hands, worship Him, letting your newly unburdened heart rejoice!

That's the order: pour, petition, praise! Then watch the Lord shower miracles into your life!

Lord, I pour out my heart to You, my Father, my God, my Rock,
and my Fortress! Give me hope, strength, and the desires
of my heart. I thank and praise You in Jesus' name!

THE TIME IS NEAR

Blessed is the one who reads aloud the words of this prophecy, and blessed are those who hear it and take to heart what is written in it, because the time is near.
REVELATION 1:3 NIV

It's so easy to get caught up in the here and now. There are bills to pay, jobs to do, kids to raise, vacations to take. . .any kind of distraction you can think of. Satan tries to keep us so busy that we don't even realize we've taken our focus off the Lord.

The Bible tells us that we are blessed if we read God's Word and take it to heart, because "the time is near"! Are you living each day with that in mind?

There are several essential principles in this verse that we shouldn't miss. First, we need to be reading God's Word each day. Strapped for time? Go to an online Bible site and have scripture e-mailed to you every day! Second, take to heart what you've read. Meditate on a few verses of scripture each day, and ask God to teach you something from them. Ask Him to help you apply His Word to your life. Third, remember that "the time is near"! Live your everyday life like Jesus might be coming back today!

Jesus, help me to keep my focus on You. Give me the time and desire to be in Your Word each day. In Your name, amen.

INTENSELY EMOTIONAL

Jesus wept.
JOHN 11:35 NIV

She was an emotional woman. Many times her passion for life was expressed with tears. She cried at her mother's death and her child's hospitalization. But she also shed tears at her granddaughter's birth and son's graduation. In celebration or sorrow, she wore her emotions on her sleeve. She embraced life by intensely feeling every hill and valley. Embarrassed by her tears as a teen, she finally learned to view her gift of passion as a blessing from the Lord.

Perhaps you, too, are an emotional woman. Take heart. Jesus wept. Although this is the shortest verse in the Bible, it speaks volumes. Jesus had emotions and was not embarrassed to express them. He cried when his good friend Lazarus died. In the Garden of Gethsemane, his soul was overwhelmed with sorrow. We read that His anger was unleashed when He drove the money changers out of the temple. Jesus cared. He felt intensely. He was passionate about life because, as the Creator, He knew that life was not happenstance. Jesus was sent to Earth for the divine purpose of redeeming fallen man. How could He not care? How could things not matter? How could He not weep?

We were created in His image. We were created to feel, to have emotions. Embrace them. Emotions are an expression of the heart. Don't be afraid to reveal your heart to others. Follow Jesus' example.

Dear Lord, thank You for creating me with emotions.
May I express them appropriately. Amen.

GOD'S GRIP

For I hold you by your right hand—I, the Lord your God.
And I say to you, "Don't be afraid. I am here to help you."
ISAIAH 41:13 NLT

Trouble comes into every life: We all lose jobs, have loved ones fall ill, and face spiritual crises. In our marriages, we experience sometimes-heated disagreements, confusion about what life direction we should take, and seemingly unsolvable dilemmas. As long as we are earthbound, unexpected and unwelcome problems remain our lot.

Often we feel tempted to ask, "Where was God when this happened?"

The answer? He was gripping our right hands, ready to help us through it all.

It's not as if God didn't see ahead to our life-distorting events. No difficulty we face comes as a surprise to Him. The Omniscient One is aware of all that lies in our futures; but charitably, He does not give us warning. He knows we'd only fuss and worry or try to work things out for ourselves and land ourselves in even bigger trouble. Instead He walks hand in hand with even the most challenged believer who reaches out for His comforting grip.

Facing trouble today? Cling to this verse, believe it, and turn your concerns over to the Lord. Don't waste time in fear and worry. Your Lord knows just where you are headed.

Lord, help me cling to Your hand and feel Your tight and loving grip.

WHAT'S YOUR FRAGRANCE?

*But thank God! He has made us his captives and continues to lead us
along in Christ's triumphal procession. Now he uses us to spread
the knowledge of Christ everywhere, like a sweet perfume.
Our lives are a Christ-like fragrance rising up to God.*
2 CORINTHIANS 2:14–15 NLT

It has been said that the average human being can detect up to ten thousand
different odors. Smells can evoke powerful images—the smell of mothballs can take
us right back to when we were eight years old and playing in Grandma's attic. The
scent of pine can transport us to the ski vacation we took in college with friends.

As followers of Christ, we have been given a very unique fragrance. And whether
we intend it to or not, our very presence in the lives of others always leaves a lingering scent. When we are kind to someone who doesn't deserve it, it smells wonderful.
When we help a person in need, the fragrance lingers long after we've gone. Paul
says that regardless of what we do, our fragrance should *always* remind people of
Christ.

As you go about your business today, what kind of fragrance will you take with
you? Pause for a moment to ask God to help you be a sweet representative of Christ,
leaving His delightful aroma lingering in the air behind you.

*Father, help me to touch, in some small way, each person I meet today.
Help me to leave behind a fragrance that reminds them of You.*

DIFFERENT

Fear not; I will do to thee all that thou requirest: for all the
city of my people doth know that thou art a virtuous woman.
RUTH 3:11 KJV

Ruth was not a nice Jewish girl. She hailed from Moab, Israel's enemy. Ruth had been exposed to idol worship, some of which may have included human sacrifice and fertility rites. When she arrived in Bethlehem with Naomi, her late husband's mother, the townspeople probably shook their heads at the way she dressed.

Yet Boaz, a prominent citizen, did not hesitate to marry Ruth. Why? Because she cared deeply for Naomi, a penniless old woman, and worked hard to provide for her. Ruth not only left her own family and culture behind but also vowed to follow Naomi's God. Boaz—and his entire hometown—soon recognized Ruth's kindness and determination to change.

Though Ruth lived more than three thousand years ago, her example of love and faithfulness is worth imitating. And when we ask for God's help in blessing those we don't understand and who don't understand us, we can be sure He will come to our aid just as He helped Ruth.

Lord God, it's not easy to adjust to others' needs.
Let the loving fragrance of my life draw them to You. Amen.

FLOATING IN GRACE

"Be still, and know that I am God."
PSALM 46:10 NIV

Sometimes we want the answers while we are still thrashing in the waves of our own doubt, but the truth is, we seldom find wisdom until we are still. When we're tossed about, the horizon may, for the moment, leave our sight. And we are lost. These are the times when we are called to stillness. For many of us, doing *something* seems better than doing *nothing*, but it is easier to see clear to the bottom of our problems after all the ripples have faded.

Silence and stillness are the doorways that welcome our weary hearts in prayer. Prayer can be full of lamenting and asking, but when we realize that deep prayer is more a quieting of the soul, the power of who God is floods into our hearts. He is order amid the chaos, the foundation of all reason, and pure goodness in an unjust world. Through this kind of prayer, loves rushes in and renews us.

God is endless and unaltered love. The God who parted the Red Sea and calmed the storms is the same God who works His grace into our everyday lives. Eternity is on the horizon. All we need to do is look to Him, and we will float in depths where our feet can't touch and walk over anything that threatens to overcome us.

Father, You calm the storms and heal my doubt. Help me begin
every day in prayer with a calm heart and stillness of mind,
that I may have a better understanding of You. Amen.

MRS. POTIPHAR

Keep watching and praying that you may not enter into temptation.
MATTHEW 26:41 NASB

Potiphar's wife had set her cap on her husband's servant. Scripture tells us that Joseph was a looker, "well-built and handsome, and after a while his master's wife took notice of Joseph and said, 'Come to bed with me!' " (Genesis 39:6–7 NIV).

But Mrs. Potiphar had underestimated Joseph's integrity. He explained that he could never betray her husband's trust. Even more indicative of Joseph's sterling nature, he said, "How then could I do such a wicked thing and sin against God?" (Genesis 39:9 NIV). Joseph's relationship with God was so well established that he knew a sin—any sin—would be an offense against God.

Mrs. Potiphar wouldn't give up. "And though she spoke to Joseph day after day, he refused to go to bed with her or even be with her" (Genesis 39:10 NIV).

Her pride wounded, Mrs. Potiphar decided to punish Joseph. She waited until the house was empty of servants so there would be no witnesses, and then she accused Joseph of rape. Her husband threw Joseph into prison.

Why prison? Potiphar had every right to have Joseph executed. Did he suspect his wife's duplicity? We never learn anything more about Mrs. Potiphar, which might be scripture's way of telling us that we know enough. She was an immoral, scheming woman who sought to harm a man of God. And yet God used her treachery for good in Joseph's life. God can use anyone or anything to accomplish His purposes.

*Lord, guard me against any tendency toward becoming
emotionally or physically involved in an off-limits relationship.
Let me be like Joseph, who stayed clear of temptation.*

YOUR TALENTS

*God has given each of you a gift from his great variety of spiritual gifts.
Use them well to serve one another.*

1 PETER 4:10 NLT

Author Leo Buscaglia said, "Your talent is God's gift to you. What you do with it is your gift back to God."

What's your talent? Is it balancing numbers, writing stories, being a homemaker, caring for others, making people laugh, baking sweets, preaching, teaching?

Not sure what your gift is? Well, what are you good at? What do you enjoy doing? What talent do you feel a burning need to share? What do you feel God leading you to do? Whatever your answer is to these questions, that's your gift.

It may be that your gift or talent is not something you can use on the job. Perhaps it's not even something from which you can make money. That's okay. Use it anyway.

If you have a way with words, write an article for your church newsletter. If you have a drive to instruct, teach a Sunday school class. If you love to cook, begin by trying out some gourmet dishes on your husband.

Use the gifts God has given you. In doing so, you will find your life blessed and, at the same time, will become a blessing to others. And, as an added bonus, you'll be giving your gift back to God. Is there anything better than that?

*Lord, I owe You so much, and although I can never truly repay You,
I can use the gifts You have given me to help others. Show me my gifts,
Lord. And help me find ways to use them. All to Your glory!*

SARAH'S DAUGHTERS

Through faith also Sara herself received strength to conceive seed,
and was delivered of a child when she was past age,
because she judged him faithful who had promised.
HEBREWS 11:11 KJV

Although the popular Narnia series by C. S. Lewis draws attention to the "daughters of Eve," this is not a biblical idea.

While we are daughters of Eve because she was the mother of all living, we are not to pattern ourselves after her. We are never told to be daughters of Eve. Rather, we are encouraged to be daughters of Sarah.

Eve was deceived and fell into transgression. But Sarah was faithful.

Sarah obeyed Abraham, even in dangerous situations.

Sarah reverenced Abraham, calling him "lord."

Even though Sarah, when told that she would have a son in her old age, had laughed at the idea and then denied doing so, she still had the faith to conceive Isaac. However little her faith was, it earned her a place in the Hall of Faith in Hebrews 11.

How can we be daughters of Sarah?

Peter tells us that we should be in subjection to our own husbands, showing them reverence. We need to display chaste behavior, focus on our inward growth rather than our outward appearance, and have a meek and quiet spirit.

These qualities are lightly esteemed in our modern world but are of priceless value to our heavenly Father. If you would honor Him, be Sarah's daughter.

Father, it sometimes goes against my flesh to be quiet, meek, and reverent to my husband. I yield myself to Your Spirit now, Father. Transform my mind. Silence my mouth. Make me Sarah's daughter. Amen.

EARTH'S DARK GLASSES

For now we see through a glass, darkly; but then face to face:
now I know in part; but then shall I know even as also I am known.
1 CORINTHIANS 13:12 KJV

She had been married for only a year. Her skin was smooth, her hair thick, her body slim and graceful. She knew her husband loved her, but sometimes she wondered if his love would be as strong when her hair was white and thin and her cheeks were sagging and spotted with age. Looking for reassurance, she studied the other couples in church on Sundays, especially one older couple who sat nearby. This husband and wife had been married for more than five decades, and the years hung heavily on them.

Week after week she watched them, and then it dawned on her. It seemed as if they did not see each other as the rest of the world did. When the wife took her husband's thin arm, she was holding the muscular arm of her young husband. When the husband smiled into his wife's face, he wasn't seeing the wrinkles and liver spots. He was seeing the young woman he married fifty years before.

Soon and very soon these bodies will be discarded and God will give us new ones. Until then, let us try to see each other—and trust that we are seen—as God sees us: spotless and without blemish, covered in the precious blood of the Lamb.

Dear Lord, help me be content with the body You have given me. Thank You
for the hope of the resurrection and a new, glorified body in the future. Amen.

ASKING FOR TROUBLE

Therefore do not worry about tomorrow, for tomorrow will worry about itself. Each day has enough trouble of its own.
MATTHEW 6:34 NIV

God's Word is very clear about worrying. God says: don't do it! Did you know that it is actually a sin to worry? When we worry, we are telling God that we don't trust Him enough with our future.

How often do we worry? Almost hourly, right? We have a lot of confessing to do then, don't we? We worry about how we're going to pay all the bills, if this person we're committed to will truly be committed to us for the rest of our lives, if we will get a life-threatening illness, and so on. We worry about so much, yet God says don't do it! How do we stop?

We have to commit our life, our plans, and our thoughts to the Lord *each day*! Make this the first thing you do every morning. The Bible tells us to give all of our worries over to the Lord because He cares for us (1 Peter 5:7). It also tells us that worrying won't add one single hour to our lives (Luke 12:25). So why do it? When we worry, we're just asking for trouble!

Father, please forgive me for worrying. Help me to trust You at all times. In Jesus' name, amen.

HONOR GOD WITH HEALTHY HABITS

When you eat or drink or do anything else,
always do it to honor God.
1 Corinthians 10:31 cev

The statistics are grim. Sixty percent of Americans are overweight or obese. Only about a third of us get the minimum recommended amount of exercise each day. Health problems that were once reserved for elderly people, like diabetes and high blood pressure, are now affecting us at younger and younger ages. In spite of living in a society obsessed with diet and exercise, many of us are becoming increasingly unhealthy. Yet the Bible says that in whatever we do we are to honor God, and that includes anything we do with our bodies (1 Corinthians 6:20). We often think of this in relation to sexual purity. And it certainly applies. However, we also have an opportunity to honor God with our bodies by taking good care of them—by getting enough rest and enough exercise.

Take a look in the mirror. You probably need at least eight hours of sleep each night so that your body can function optimally. Do you make it a priority to get enough rest, or do you stretch yourself to the limit all week and then try to make up for it on the weekends? The surgeon general recommends that adults get thirty to sixty minutes of physical activity most days of the week. Is there time in your day for fresh air and exercise? Particularly as you age, healthy habits are an investment that will pay enormous dividends down the road. It sounds like a cliché, but you only get one body—make it a priority to honor God with it.

Father, thank You for blessing me with a body that does so much for me.
Please help me to make it a priority to care for it in a way that honors You. Amen.

BECOMING A FOLLOWER

I will instruct you and teach you in the way
you should go; I will guide you with My eye.
PSALM 32:8 NKJV

Sometimes life can seem to be careening out of control, so much so that you feel like a firefighter running from here to there, extinguishing the fires breaking out in your life or the lives of those around you. Distractions, crises, and interruptions try their best to rob you of your peace, energy, and strength.

But when you accepted Jesus as your Lord and Savior, you were turned inside out. You have the ability to live from your spirit instead of your emotions. The Spirit of God within you wants to guide you and give you something that can't come from your emotions alone—daily peace.

Relax and let the real you—your spirit—lead and guide you in all truth. Instead of reacting to your circumstances, stop and respond to the voice of God. Then perhaps you'll still put out fires, but you'll arrive on the scene when the blaze is more manageable, with a clear sense of what needs to be done to bring about the best outcome for your life and the lives of those around you.

Heavenly Father, I want to respond to life, not react to it.
Help me to hear Your voice and follow Your lead. Amen.

WORD OR DEED

*And whatever you do, whether in word or deed, do it all in the name
of the Lord Jesus, giving thanks to God the Father through him.*
COLOSSIANS 3:17 NIV

There is no such thing as a Sunday Christian. Bearing the name of Christ is a twenty-four-hour, seven-day-a-week proposition. Whether we're working, shopping at the grocery store, or playing golf, our lives reflect the One we profess. Once we are united with Christ, our secular and spiritual lives are also united. We should not live one way during the week and then act differently at church on Sunday. People are watching. Inconsistency is quickly recognized. Hypocrisy is offensive.

Although Christians are far from perfect, we are called to be Christ's ambassadors, His representatives. In a world filled with darkness, we have the privilege of being light to those who are lost. By reflecting His glory, we proclaim His truth: Jesus Christ is the way, the truth, and the life (John 14:6).

So whatever you do or say, represent Jesus well. May He be your focus so that others will be drawn to Him. Allow Jesus access to every part of your life, every day of your life. Don't hide your light under a bushel. Let it shine brightly to a world that is lost.

May the light of Christ in you be clearly seen by others. Christ in you is indeed the hope of glory!

*Dear Lord, may I represent You as I should.
May my words and actions be pleasing to You. Amen.*

DAILY BREAD

Give us today our daily bread.
MATTHEW 6:11 NIV

In our mega warehouse culture, buying in bulk has become a trend that carries over into the rest of our lives. Who can argue that storing up on dish soap and paper towels doesn't bring some sense of security to our anxious hearts? So, with our pantries full, we look toward the unknown with hope for similar assurances. In our spiritual lives, this is an entirely different matter indeed—our hands and hearts need to be emptied before they can be filled. God gives us just enough for one day.

The truth is that no matter what false securities we create, it is God who takes us into tomorrow. In our sleep, God refreshes and renews us so that each morning we have what we need to face the new day's demands. His grace is not something we can stockpile but rather something we give away.

Whenever we feel our hearts tighten over outcomes we want, we simply need to loosen our grip and rest in Him. Because we live in a world of independence and self-sufficiency, this faith feels awkward at first until we experience a joy unmatched by anything we can conjure up on our own. It is in these divine moments that we can throw open the cupboard doors of our heart and give away everything that's there, knowing that tomorrow we will be full again.

Father, thank You for giving us our manna each and every day.
Thank You for providing for all our needs as we continually reap the
joy of knowing You as the trustworthy sustainer of our lives. Amen.

PERSONALIZED PRAYER

I have hidden your word in my heart.
PSALM 119:11 NLT

Lots of Bible verses contain the words *he*, *him*, and *his*. One reason for that is that most of the Bible stories are about men and the deeds they performed, the prayers they prayed, the psalms they wrote and sang. Another reason is that the scriptures—Old and New—were written from the perspective of a male-dominated society. As a result, sometimes it's hard for us women to get close to a verse, to take it to heart when the references were made to males and we are definitely females. So what's a girl to do?

Make it personal. If there is a verse that's really speaking to your heart, one that you'd like to commit to memory so that you can pull it from the recesses of your mind when needed, write it down using *she*, *her*, or *hers* (or, for that matter, *I, you,* and *we*) where appropriate.

For example, a great verse to store away for those less-than-peaceful moments is Isaiah 26:3. In the New King James Version, the verse reads, "You will keep him in perfect peace, whose mind is stayed on You, because he trusts in You." Make this personal by changing it to "You will keep *her* in perfect peace, whose mind is stayed on You, because *she* trusts in You." Or better yet, "You will keep *me* in perfect peace, whose mind is stayed on You, because *I* trust in You."

It's God's Word meant for you. So truly take it to heart by making it your very own. Make it personal. Because if God is nothing else, He's personal.

Lord, I want to make Your Word truly mine. Help me to understand,
to make Your Word personal. Let's talk. . .heart to heart.

MAKING BREAD

*Be humble under God's powerful hand so
he will lift you up when the right time comes.*
1 PETER 5:6 NCV

When we reach the end of everything we know, that is when God rolls up His sleeves and does His best work in our lives. He waits until we are finished rolling our problems around like dough, pounding away until there is nothing left to be done. When we hand our mess over to Him with humble and sticky fingers, He takes it all and transforms it into a kind of bread that nourishes us.

There is a story about orphaned children during WWII who were left homeless and starving. Once rescued, they had trouble sleeping at night out of fear that they would wake in the morning and be hungry again. After all attempts were made to ease their fears, someone came up with the idea of giving each child a piece of bread to hold during the night. It worked. The children slept peacefully, holding their bread. We can take a lesson from those children and hold our bread as a symbol that God was with us today and will be with us again tomorrow.

The art of spiritual bread making requires a deep patience that allows obstacles to rest, quietly covered in His grace, so that they can rise into opportunities that give us strength. He works in miracles—turning even our most difficult ordeals into blessings that can heal us.

*Father, You are the Bread of Life. Give us the faith and the
patience we need to allow You to work in our lives. Amen.*

BUSIER THAN THE PRIME MINISTER OF BABYLON?

Three times a day [Daniel] got down on his knees and prayed,
giving thanks to his God, just as he had done before.
DANIEL 6:10 NIV

Like clockwork, Daniel had a custom of praying three times a day. He left his office, went home, and knelt by an open window that faced Jerusalem. Taken from Judah as a young teenager and forced into "friendly captivity" by King Nebuchadnezzar of Babylon, Daniel excelled in his responsibilities. In return, he was treated well and rose through the ranks of Babylon bureaucracy. Eventually he became one of three "prime ministers" of Babylon! And still he knew who he was, and he knew who his God was. He never forgot.

Are we praying faithfully for the people God has placed in our lives? Most likely, our record of praying for them is spotty at best. But are we any busier than a prime minister of Babylon? Daniel made a habit of regular, effective prayer. It was just as important to him as food—maybe more so.

We need to develop effective prayer habits for our friends and family. Prayer doesn't have to be locked to a time or a place or a particular posture. We need to kneel in our hearts whenever we sense the Lord's inner promptings to pray.

Lord, forgive me for growing complacent in prayer. Poke me!
Wake me! Remind me to pray regularly for my family,
for their hearts to belong to You for all eternity.

INSIDE OUT

*In like manner also, that women adorn themselves in modest apparel,
with shamefacedness and sobriety; not with broided hair, or gold, or pearls,
or costly array; but (which becometh women professing godliness) with good works.*
1 TIMOTHY 2:9-10 KJV

Is it wrong to have a desire to look nice? No! Are women required to walk around looking at the ground? Absolutely not. The point of this verse is not that women should do their best to look frumpy and unattractive. It *is*, however, to point out that being well dressed and expensively adorned is completely pointless if inner beauty is absent.

It is possible to be neatly, even stylishly, attired and still be modest. Your makeup and jewelry can be applied neatly and with good taste, but it should not be done in a way that draws unnecessary attention to yourself.

Your purpose is to be godly—to draw people to Jesus. You do this by walking so closely with Him that His beauty is reflected in You. All your designer clothes and expensive accessories are worthless—an artificial beauty—if Christ's love is not radiating through your entire being.

Get your priorities straight. Be sure your heart is beautiful, and external attractiveness is sure to follow.

*Lord Jesus, let Your love shine through me.
May my heart be beautiful in Your sight.*

FREELY GIVE

Freely you have received; freely give.
MATTHEW 10:8 NIV

As women, we're accustomed to devoting ourselves to do—and be—as many things as others need. Giving, for us, is as natural as breathing. That is, until we find that we are dancing delicately on a tightrope in a precarious balancing act between what we need and what others want. Despite all our efforts, gravity usually wins as the truth comes crashing down. We simply can't give what we don't have.

It was never God's plan that we spin through life with nothing but a bag of tricks to get us by. Talent and caffeinated energy only work for so long until the moment comes when we reach into our empty pockets and conclude that we have nothing else to give.

Generous giving begins when we dig into the soil of God's sustenance and find what He has planted for us. We are nourished by this precious truth of who we are in Christ. He fills us with unlimited resources of love, patience, wisdom, and truth. From this place, we are free to give without fear of falling or becoming empty.

Every day the questions laid out before us are these: How can we enter into our day without being connected to the Source who offers His love like a spring? How can we attend to the myriad of demands placed on us without freely accepting the power that God offers first?

Father, help me to begin each day in Your Word so that I can be filled with the Holy Spirit and give from Your strength rather than my own. Amen.

FEMALE ISSUES

He said to her, "Daughter, be of good cheer;
your faith has made you well. Go in peace."
LUKE 8:48 NKJV

When it comes time for prayer requests, nothing can clear a room faster than a woman revealing she has "female problems." Even our husbands are sometimes embarrassed when we want to discuss womanly issues that they can't even begin to fathom. Yet Jesus didn't waver when "a woman having an issue of blood twelve years" (Luke 8:43 KJV) came to Him for help. Talk about issues!

This was one brave woman, considering that Leviticus 15:19 made it clear that any female with an issue of blood was to be set apart from everyone else for seven days. She was deemed "unclean," and anything she'd even *touch* would turn unclean.

Yet this particular physically weak woman, who was full of faith, boldly approached the Great Physician, knowing that if she just touched Him, she would be healed!

When she felt Jesus' garment, some of His power left Him and immediately healed her! When He realized what had happened, He wasn't embarrassed or repulsed. In fact, Jesus responded with wonderful words: "Daughter, be of good cheer; your faith has made you well. Go in peace." Ah, words to live by. Words that heal.

If you have an "issue" that you are reluctant to share with others, take your faith and bring it to Jesus. He's waiting for you to receive His power, to be healed, to find peace.

Lord, thank You for allowing me, Your daughter, to share everything with You.
I come to You with my issues and am ready to receive
Your power, blessing, and peace.

TRANSPARENCY

*Do not conform to the pattern of this world, but be transformed
by the renewing of your mind. Then you will be able to test and approve
what God's will is—his good, pleasing and perfect will.*
ROMANS 12:2 NIV

Lack of communication skills is one of the greatest hindrances to healthy relationships. Most of the time when we pray, we are seeking change. We cannot change others, but we *can* submit to God's design for our lives through the transformation of the Holy Spirit.

Your words are powerful! They shape the atmosphere of your home and the hearts of all who enter. Your very words build up or tear down relationships. Take a breath and realize that your husband and children have a right to express themselves. Make room for their ideas and opinions even when they are different than yours.

Allow yourself to become transparent to God. Ask God to reveal the real *you* to you. When we allow Him to expose the truth of who we are, He brings everything to the light. When we are reproved by His love, then our weaknesses are made visible and He is able to heal the past wounds and hurts that have controlled our behavior and speech.

Focus your words on building up, and when you do need to speak a difficult word, ask the Lord to help you say it with His love.

*Lord, teach me to guard my heart with all diligence, and show
me how to speak the truth in love in my home, in my church,
with my friends, and in all my relationships. Amen.*

GOOD THINGS

And the people spake against God, and against Moses, Wherefore have ye brought us up out of Egypt to die in the wilderness? for there is no bread, neither is there any water; and our soul loatheth this light bread.

NUMBERS 21:5 KJV

At this point in their journey of deliverance, the Israelites had seen many miracles. They had followed a cloud and a pillar of fire and had been fed with manna. They had seen the Red Sea part (or had heard about it). More recently they had seen the earth open to swallow up their rebellious brothers.

Yet when the going got tough and they were without real bread and fresh water, they complained against God. In fact, they said they *hated* what God had supplied!

We look back at them and are amazed. How could they be so dense, so faithless? God was obviously with them. How could they possibly doubt His love and care for them?

But are we any better?

Believers have the indwelling Holy Spirit. God is *in* us; He is always with us. He has promised to never forsake us.

Yet when the going gets tough—when our finances and relationships are strained and when we don't have what we think we need—we complain just as the Israelites did.

Let us learn the lessons they did not. Let us trust in our Father, knowing that He cares and is always working for our good.

How often I complain about the little irritations and miss seeing all the good things You give me, Father. Have mercy on my fickle heart. Amen.

FIRST THINGS FIRST

*In the morning, LORD, you hear my voice; in the morning
I lay my requests before you and wait expectantly.*
PSALM 5:3 NIV

No team takes the field without first meeting in the locker room for a pregame talk. No actor takes the stage without first getting into character. It would be foolish to build a house without consulting with an architect and drawing up plans. For any successful endeavor, preparation is key.

Throughout His earthly ministry, Jesus modeled this principle. He was an incredibly busy Man. There were disciples to train, people to heal, and children to bless. No matter what He did or where He traveled, something or someone always seemed to need attention. However, in spite of the many demands placed upon Him, scripture tells us that Jesus got up early in the morning, while it was still dark, and took time to meet His Father in prayer (Mark 1:35). Jesus was perfect, and yet even He knew this discipline was essential to ensuring the effectiveness of His ministry.

What is the first thing you do each morning? Many of us hit the ground running, armed with to-do lists a mile long. Unfortunately, this means we try to take off in a hundred different directions, lacking focus, falling into our beds each night with a sense that we haven't accomplished anything at all.

While it doesn't ensure perfection, setting aside a short time each morning to focus on the Father and the day ahead can help prepare us to live more intentionally. In these moments we, like Jesus, gain clarity so that we can invest our lives in the things that truly matter.

*Father, help me to take time each morning to focus on You and the day ahead.
Align my priorities so that the things I do will be the things You want me to do.*

SERVING THE LORD

Whatever you do, work at it with all your heart, as working for the Lord,
not for human masters, since you know that you will receive an inheritance
from the Lord as a reward. It is the Lord Christ you are serving.
COLOSSIANS 3:23–24 NIV

God has given all of us some work to accomplish. Whether it's a daily job, raising a family, taking care of a home and a business. . .some of our tasks tend to be tiresome jobs that we wish we could hire someone else to do.

As Christians in today's society, we really need to change our thinking about our little jobs. We need to keep Colossians 3:23–24 in mind anytime we are working so that Christ will be glorified. If we take these verses to heart, our attitudes will change and we will be a strong witness to others.

Try getting up five minutes earlier this week and spending that time memorizing these verses. Write them down and ask the Lord to change your heart and attitude about any grunt work you don't usually enjoy doing. You will see a change in your life and marriage as you take these verses to heart. Your attitude at home will be much better as you mop the floor and clean the toilets because you are doing these tasks as an act of worship to the Lord!

Dear Lord, I want to worship You in everything I do. Change my attitude about
the little things so that I may be a good witness to You always. Amen.

SACRED GROUND

Until now you have not asked for anything in my name.
Ask and you will receive, and your joy will be complete.
JOHN 16:24 NIV

Every day, Jesus invites us to enter into a holy place with Him by praying in His name. So often we ask for things in our daily rush from here to there: "Lord, please give me a parking space close to the door." Or things that do require some miracle making: "Please change my husband." Certainly these prayers, if answered, would make our lives easier, but Jesus isn't talking about prayers that simply make us happier. He is talking about prayers that bring us complete and utter joy.

When we step out of ourselves and into a life with Jesus, we begin to see how this mystery of joy unfolds. Over time, His words take root and weave into our own, until we find ourselves unsure where His thoughts end and ours begin.

And one rainy day in a crowded parking lot, you see a woman you've never met but suddenly know she needs help getting to her car. Or you gain new insight into the pressure your husband is under and feel tenderness toward him you haven't felt before. In those moments of clarity when our words and prayers become one with Jesus', the sacred ground on which we walk is the ten steps it takes to offer an umbrella, an extra hand, or a loving embrace.

Father, teach me how to enter into a relationship with You so deeply that I can hear Your voice and feel Your joy as I pray Your words as my own. Amen.

TIMING IS EVERYTHING

*"Go and gather together all the Jews of Susa and fast for me. Do not eat
or drink for three days, night or day. My maids and I will do the same.
And then, though it is against the law, I will go in to see the king."*
ESTHER 4:16 NLT

Esther was an orphan in a foreign land. Suddenly she found herself on center stage as King Xerxes of Persia's new bride. Barely accustomed to her new duties as queen, Esther faced a crisis of enormous proportions. She learned that the king had unwittingly placed all Jews living in Persia, including herself, in jeopardy. Prior to risking her life for her people, she humbled herself by fasting and asking for prayer support from others.

How did God direct her? To wait patiently for the right time to speak. In ancient times, the queen risked her life by appearing in front of the king's throne unless she was summoned. Esther had something she needed to say to King Xerxes, but she paused and prayed and proceeded cautiously and carefully. Xerxes saw her standing in the hall. Pleased, he was in a mood eager to give Esther anything she wanted. Timing was everything.

This is a wise reminder for us to choose our words carefully and to deliver those words at the right time. We want our message to be well received. Is our husband hungry? Tired? Irritable? Distracted? Those aren't the moments for heart-to-heart conversation. What we say matters—but so do how and when.

*Lord, give me Esther's restraint. Make me sensitive to Your guidance.
May I learn to practice instant obedience.*

HUMILITY BRINGS GLORY

For all those who exalt themselves will be humbled,
and those who humble themselves will be exalted.
LUKE 14:11 NIV

The tree was bare. Every leaf had been shed. Winter had arrived. Yet beyond the barren tree, the sun peeked its head above the treetops. Dawn was breaking. As the sun ascended higher, its rays were visible through the bare branches. Before long, the entire tree was glowing as the sun's radiance shone through it.

Many times our lives seem barren, as if we've been stripped of everything. We find ourselves humbled, humiliated, forsaken, or rejected—standing alone, like a barren tree. But our story does not end there. God's glory will burst forth. Wait. At just the right time, like the sunrise, He makes His appearance. When He does, His light will shine through because our branches are bare. The world will see. Our humility allows others to see the Lord clearly through us because the focus is no longer on us but on Him. When we decrease, the Lord will increase.

Do not view humility with disdain. His glory can only be revealed when we are humble. Humble yourself before the Lord, and He will lift you up. He will shine through you. You will reflect and make known His glory. May it be so!

Dear Lord, may humility characterize my
life so that You may be glorified. Amen.

MICHAL'S CHOICE

As the ark of the Lord was entering the City of David, Michal daughter of Saul watched from a window. And when she saw King David leaping and dancing before the Lord, she despised him in her heart.

2 SAMUEL 6:16 NIV

Nine years earlier, Michal was hopelessly in love with David. She even betrayed her father, King Saul, to save David's life. But today, that love was dead. His effervescent joy only embarrassed her.

Michal couldn't identify with David's joy because she didn't share it. She had no appreciation for the significance of the return of the ark of the Lord to Jerusalem. But to David, it meant basking in the presence of the Lord.

When David returned home, Michal met him at the door, eyes blazing. She blasted him with hot hatred! And he responded by distancing himself from her.

Like most couples, Michal and David once loved each other passionately, but nine stressful years later, that passion had died. Instead of replacing her emptiness with God, Michal let her heart remain. . .empty.

We think passion will be enough to sustain a marriage, but it isn't. Only God can satisfy our heart's deepest desires.

It could have been so different for Michal! She was David's first love. She could have been his last one.

Make God your first choice. Allow Him to fill your heart. He'll keep your love alive!

Lord, may I have a heart like David. He seemed to intuitively understand that You belonged first in his life.

THE DAWN OF MOURNING

Blessed are those who mourn, for they will be comforted.
MATTHEW 5:4 NIV

When dreams become shadows and sadness tramples our hearts, mourning becomes the way we learn to breathe again. It is sanity, really, that prompts us to cry out and break the silence that simply absorbs our loss. Giving voice to our grief joins us in song with all those who have suffered before. It releases our sadness and keeps it from settling into and numbing our hearts.

We mourn many things throughout our life. . .loss of loved ones, our health, our ideas, or our expectations. But bemoaning our earthly losses is not the type of mourning Jesus is talking about in the Beatitudes. He is referring to what happens when we are hit with the overwhelming realization that we are spiritually lost beings in need of a Savior. Simply put, we are the walking dead, living a useless life over a fixed amount of time. And the clock is running.

Jesus says that those who grieve over their desperate spiritual condition are blessed. Yes, *blessed*, because He has great news! He offers us everlasting life with Him through His Son, Jesus. He gives the dead new life. Every time we stumble in sin and fall on our pain, He promises to comfort us and restore us to Him. His love and complete forgiveness turn our mourning into a new day.

Father, thank You for the comfort You give me when I can't
help but see myself as I really am. Thank You for Your
forgiveness and promise of everlasting life. Amen.

RUN HOME

But now, GOD's Message, the God who made you in the first place,
Jacob, the One who got you started, Israel: "Don't be afraid,
I've redeemed you. I've called your name. You're mine."
ISAIAH 43:1 MSG

Remember when you were a child and you ran outside to play? When it came time for dinner, your mom called you in. She called you by name. And you stopped whatever you were doing and ran. You ran home. Because at home, your parents (the ones whose love created you) protected you and provided for you. They fed, clothed, and nourished you. They answered all your questions. They gave you direction.

Now you're all grown up. And there is still One who protects you, provides for you, and nourishes you. It's God, the One who got you started. He calls you by your name. You are His! He longs for you to run home to Him!

Listen! Be still. Quiet your thoughts. Do you hear Him? He's calling your name!

Drop whatever you're doing and run! Run into His arms. Allow Him to fill you with His Spirit and peace. Allow Him to love you with an everlasting love. Allow Him to feed you with His Word. Allow Him to hold you tight. He will never let you fall, never let you go. You need not be afraid. You're home!

Lord, I hear You calling my name! Here I am, Lord!
Here I am! I'm coming home!

THE MASTER MULTIPLIER

And they said to Him, "We have here only five loaves and two fish."
MATTHEW 14:17 NKJV

One day five thousand people were sitting on a hillside, listening to Jesus. But as the day drew to a close, stomachs began to growl. Knowing that they were faced with an inordinate amount of hungry mouths, the disciples panicked, telling Jesus to send the crowd away to buy bread from the surrounding villages.

But Jesus said to them, "You give them something to eat" (Mark 6:37 NKJV).

This, to the disciples, seemed like an impossibility! Focusing on what they lacked, the disciples knew there was no way five loaves and two fish would satisfy this hungry mob. Yet Jesus commanded them to bring their meager stores to Him.

Then Jesus "took the five loaves and the two fish, and looking up to heaven, He blessed and broke and gave the loaves to the disciples; and the disciples gave to the multitudes" (Matthew 14:19 NKJV). And here's the amazing thing: "They all ate and were filled" (Matthew 14:20 NKJV)! Not only that, but they ended up with twelve baskets filled with leftovers!

With Jesus in our lives, we dare not look at what we lack—in our marriage, our family, our job, or our church. Instead, He wants us to take what we have and give it to Him. If we do so, He will bless our meager store and multiply it. And in the end, we will find we have more than enough!

*Jesus, help me focus not on what I lack but on what I have.
I know that You can do the impossible. So please take my
meager store, and bless and multiply it, to Your glory!*

WHAT GOD DOESN'T SEE

He hath not beheld iniquity in Jacob, neither hath he seen perverseness in Israel:
the LORD his God is with him, and the shout of a king is among them.
NUMBERS 23:21 KJV

Try as he might, Balaam could not curse the children of Israel. Instead, he blessed them.

While God had control of Balaam's wicked mouth, he made an unbelievable statement: God had not beheld iniquity in Jacob or seen perverseness in Israel.

Really? Just a few chapters earlier, Korah, Dathan, and Abiram had rebelled, and the earth had swallowed them up. Then the Israelites despised the gift of manna again, and God judged them with serpents.

There was obvious rebellion and wickedness among the people, but God said He had not beheld iniquity or perverseness in His people! How is this possible? The next statement explains this: "The LORD his God is with him."

God is with His chosen people. He sets His love upon them. He imputes His righteousness to them. Because God was in the midst of Israel, when He looked on them, He didn't see their sin—He saw Himself.

Likewise, when God looks upon His chosen now, He doesn't see our sin. He sees Himself. He sees Christ's righteousness, imputed to us through the death and resurrection of Jesus. "Blessed. . .[are] the people whom he hath chosen for his own inheritance" (Psalm 33:12 KJV).

Father, You have chosen me, saved me, sealed me, and declared me righteous.
I want to yield my whole self to You as a servant of righteousness.
Show me where I should serve You today. Amen.

WHERE ARE YOU?

They heard the sound of the LORD God walking in the garden in the cool of the day,
and the man and his wife hid themselves from the presence of the LORD God....
Then the LORD God called to the man, and said to him, "Where are you?"
GENESIS 3:8–9 NASB

Imagine having a meeting place with God every day at the same time. He waits for each of us in our favorite place—in the shade under a tree or in the coziest chair by the fireplace. For Adam and Eve, it was in the garden in the cool of the day, after the sun made its steady decline.

One day, they were gone. The tragedy of sin filled them with shame and fear so great that they hid. He called out to them, for He knows that disease grows in the dark and hidden places of our hearts. "Where are you?" was not a question of their whereabouts, but rather the cry of a Father longing for His children to come out of hiding and back into the healing light.

Now He calls to us. "Where are you?" Busy days have turned into weeks of silence. *It's been too long,* we think. *I've drifted too far.* But with God, no distance is too great. He has already gone to the ends of the earth to reach us and has died on a cross to save us.

Father, it is hard to believe that You, the Creator of the universe,
long to spend time with me every day. Help me hear Your call to come
out of my busyness or despair and spend time in Your Word. Amen.

DIVINE LOVE

So now I am giving you a new commandment: Love each other.
Just as I have loved you, you should love each other.
JOHN 13:34 NLT

It sounds simple, but rarely is it easy. Loving the people in our lives is often our toughest assignment. Isn't that why a part of us is always searching for other people to love who seem less burdensome and more deserving? Many times the behavior of those we live with stirs up confusion and sadness in us. For we each carry a lifetime of experience inside that tells us the painful truth about people. Whether it happens today or years from now, eventually they will let us down.

It is hard to avoid the clarity of Jesus' message to love people to the extent that He loves. Since God is the creator of love, He is the standard by which we are measured. He loves sacrificially, completely, and passionately, without keeping a record of past failures. Can we really love others the way God loves us? Can we love our husbands like that? Try it for just one day; it is easy to see why we need a Savior in the first place.

We may think, *Well, it would be easier if he didn't leave his towel on the floor or slam the kitchen cupboards and doors at every turn.* It's true. Our husbands can make loving them a challenge. But Jesus isn't saying that we should love our husbands as *they* deserve; we should love them in the way *He* deserves to be loved.

Father, help me to love my husband the way You do.
Please show me how. Amen.

THE DEVIL'S TRIANGLE

*For all that is in the world, the lust of the flesh, and the lust of the eyes,
and the pride of life, is not of the Father, but is of the world.*
1 JOHN 2:16 KJV

For all the complaining we do about the things we don't have, we sure miss out on a lot of the blessings from the things we do have. Our prayers are more focused on complaining to God than they are on praising Him. Why is this? Often it's because we're trapped in the devil's triangle. Our hearts are filled more with lust for things we don't possess and with sinful pride than with love for God and others and joy in the blessings He has bestowed on us.

The lust of the flesh doesn't have to trap you, though. Be aware that it is present, and arm your heart against it. As humans we *are* susceptible, but as Christians we *can* overcome. We must engross ourselves in the Word of God and let the Holy Spirit do a work in us. We need to daily crucify the old natures within us and let Jesus form us into new creatures. Once our hearts are habitually filled with true praise to our Creator, it will be easier to live in His love rather than in the lust of the devil.

Father, I praise You for Your greatness, for You alone are worthy.

HEAVEN'S EXCHANGE

For by one sacrifice he has made perfect
forever those who are being made holy.
HEBREWS 10:14 NIV

It sounds like a riddle, but it's true. We are a living work in progress all the while the final work in us has already been finished. We are forgiven and spiritually perfect at the same time we are living through the process. When this becomes too much to comprehend, just remember that we live inside Earth's time bubble, separate from eternity.

Jesus has completed the work needed to guarantee our future in heaven by dying on the cross for our sins. He has made us complete in Him by beating death and rising from the tomb. He stands in our place with a sinless record and trades our life's work with His. Because of that heavenly exchange, we are free to become who we were created to be here on Earth.

Too often we are fooled into not trusting this promise, believing that what Jesus has done is not enough and that we must take matters into our own hands. We have been trained to find ways to secure our future and earn our own way, but Jesus tells us that in life's greatest ambition, we have already won the ultimate prize.

So before you face the day ahead with all its troubles, reflect on the power of this verse. Our strength lies in accepting its truth and living as we really are in Christ.

Father, thank You for taking my place on the cross and securing for me eternal life.
Help me believe that You have completed a good work in me. Amen.

A HOLY LONGING

As the deer pants for streams of water, so my soul pants for you, my God.
My soul thirsts for God, for the living God. When can I go and meet with God?
PSALM 42:1–2 NIV

When you think of the word *longing*, what images come to mind? We long for so many things, don't we? We long for someone to love us, to tell us how special we are. We long for financial peace. We long for a great job, the perfect place to live, and even the ideal friends.

God's greatest desire is that we long for Him. Today's scripture presents a pretty clear image. We should be hungering and thirsting after God. When we've been away from Him, even for a short time, our souls should pant for Him.

If we were completely honest with ourselves, we'd have to admit that our earthly longings usually supersede our longing for God. Sure, we enjoy our worship time, but we don't really come into it with the depth of longing referred to in this scripture. Ask God to give you His perspective on longing. He knows what it means to long for someone, after all. His longing for you was so great that He gave His only Son on a cross to be near you.

Father, my earthly longings usually get in the way of my spiritual ones.
Draw me into Your presence, God. Reignite my longing for You.

LIVING THIS DAY

Therefore do not worry about tomorrow,
for tomorrow will worry about itself.
MATTHEW 6:34 NIV

So many things race through our minds: What will the next day or week or month hold? How will the test results turn out? How am I going to meet the needs of the rest of my family? When can I find some time for myself so I can regroup? Before long, our attention has shifted from the real needs of the present to the unrealized fears of another day.

God doesn't want us borrowing trouble from the future. He wants us to see how He's meeting our needs on this particular day. When we're busy projecting our worries on the days ahead, we miss what He's doing in our lives right now.

Think back to a day when you wondered how you'd have strength to get from sunrise to sunset. But you did it because God gave you His power—not for tomorrow or next month, but right when you needed it.

God knows each day has its issues. But He told us not to worry, because when the next day comes He'll be right there again, ready to equip us for whatever we need to do.

God is *your* caregiver. Let Him minister to you *this* day.

God, I'm glad that You only ask me to think upon this day. I needn't worry because
You know my needs and will meet them according to Your will.

THE ULTIMATE CAREGIVER

Casting all your care upon him; for he careth for you.
1 PETER 5:7 KJV

God is in the caregiving business. From the moment we each entered the world, He's taken care of us by meeting our needs, working tirelessly on our behalf, and shaping us into the men and women He longs for us to be. And He still cares for us—truly, passionately, intently. His great love, even when we don't deserve it, shows how much He cares.

Without question, the Lord is the ultimate caregiver. He's the best in the business. And that should motivate us as we set out to care for others. If we imitate God—not just in actions and deeds, but with our motives and intents—we can't go wrong. And when we feel overwhelmed, He has encouraged us to cast our cares on Him. Why? Because He cares so very much for us!

So run to the Lord with your struggles. Trust your heavenly Father to brush away every tear, wash away every pain, and then set you on your feet again—to care for others.

Dear Lord, as I seek to become the best I can be at what I do,
help me to keep my eyes on You. Remind me that
You were—and are—the ultimate caregiver.

IMPOSSIBLE DAYS

Out of my distress I called on the Lord;
the Lord answered me and set me free.
PSALM 118:5 ESV

Life is physically, emotionally, and spiritually draining. As we put forth all our effort, we may wonder, *Will I have enough strength to complete this task?*

When our bodies and spirits weaken, our prayers—even the most desperate ones—often become more powerful. In our emptiness, as we ask, *Lord, how much more can I bear?* He comes immediately to our aid.

God knows every need of His overburdened people. And though we may not be able to spend much time in Bible study, church attendance, and prayer, He still watches over us, listening carefully for our most helpless communications. Then He answers powerfully, in ways He may never have responded in less demanding times.

We don't need to pray perfectly or read six chapters of scripture a day before caring for our loved ones. Nor do we need to give up all our sparse personal time. God knows the service we provide, and He blesses us for it—perhaps well beyond what we feel we deserve.

The One whose "steadfast love endures forever" (Psalm 118:4 ESV) never deserts those He loves. He sets us free—even in the midst of our many chores, responsibilities, and impossible days. We can call on Him and feel His freedom no matter what our days include.

Thank You, Lord, for listening and responding to all my troubles.

CRYING OUT

I am worn out from my groaning. All night long I flood my
bed with weeping and drench my couch with tears.
PSALM 6:6 NIV

Crying is an important emotional release, but how often do we suppress our tears? Maybe we think crying indicates we're giving up hope. Or perhaps we're afraid others may think we're weak. Then there's the false notion that crying means we're not trusting God to handle our situation.

Like a cut that must be cleaned in order to heal properly, our wounded hearts need a cleansing, too. Releasing our tears to God is a way we can purify our hearts from the emotional debris collecting inside.

Our Lord set an example for us to follow. Jesus, the creator of tears, cried. He wept in front of others. He cried out to His Father. Neither fear nor pride stopped Him from expressing these painful emotions. Jesus knew that His Father would hear His cries and come to His aid.

God will do the same for us, wiping away our tears and healing the wounds of our heart. Crying may make us feel vulnerable—but God's comfort reminds us we're loved.

Dear Father, I pray I am never too scared or too proud to bring my tears
to You. How comforting it is to know You're going to dry them for me.

ALONE?

*And he took the mantle of Elijah that fell from him, and smote the waters,
and said, Where is the LORD God of Elijah? and when he also had smitten
the waters, they parted hither and thither: and Elisha went over.*

2 KINGS 2:14 KJV

For years, Elisha devoted time and energy to Elijah the prophet. He dreaded the end of his master's ministry. When the "sons of the prophets," Elijah's disciples, predicted his exit, Elisha refused to listen. When Elijah himself tried to take leave of his aide, Elisha said, "No way."

He watched miracles he did not want to see. First, Elijah parted the Jordan River with a slap of his mantle. Then a chariot of fire carried Elijah to heaven. Elisha could only cry, "My father, my father" (2 Kings 2:12 KJV), and tear his clothes in grief. His future loomed empty and sad without his mentor and friend.

But Elisha had asked for a double inheritance from his spiritual father, a twofold portion of God's Spirit. So when Elisha slapped the Jordan with his mentor's mantle and yelled, "Where is the LORD God of Elijah?" (2 Kings 2:14 KJV), the Lord parted the river again.

When we have devoted our lives to loved ones—especially those who nurtured us spiritually—we may find it difficult to go on without them. But God is still there, ready to empower us with His love so we can accomplish His purposes.

*Lord, although I'll miss the dear one I've served,
You'll send me others to love. Help me see them with Your vision.*

WONDERS OF MUSIC

But I will sing of your strength, in the morning I will sing of your love;
for you are my fortress, my refuge in times of trouble....
I sing praise to you...my God on whom I can rely.
PSALM 59:16–17 NIV

Talk about trouble—David had more than his fair share of it. Day in and day out, year after year, David was a wanted man pursued by a jealous king. Homeless, on the run, accompanied by a bunch of lowlifes, David lays out an interesting pattern in the psalms.

First, he cries out to God in sorrow, complaint, even occasional whining. But invariably, he then shifts to joyful praise.

We can be that real with God, too. We can tell Him our hearts' burdens and vent our hurts, disappointments, and struggles to Him. He can handle it.

David didn't try to sound "spiritual." He was genuine with God. Once he had cleared the air, his heart turned to thanksgiving and praise. He'd bring out the instruments, write a song or two, and regain his strength.

Music can be a source of strength to a weary soul. Whistling, humming, or singing a song of praise can help refocus a grumbling heart and restore hope when it's been waning.

Today, fill your world with songs of praise and worship.

Mighty Father, I thank You for the wonder of music. Help me to sing Your praises—
of Your strength and love daily—for You are my refuge.

GOOD WORKS ARE ALL AROUND

Well reported of for good works; if [a widow] have brought up children,
if she have lodged strangers, if she have washed the saints' feet, if she
have relieved the afflicted, if she have diligently followed every good work.
1 TIMOTHY 5:10 KJV

Often when we read the Bible, we miss its practicality. In Ephesians 2:10, for example, Paul tells us that we are created for "good works, which God hath before ordained that we should walk in them" (KJV).

How many times do we read this and wonder, *What good works am I supposed to do for God?* We may spend hours in prayer laboring to find God's will and to discover the works we are to do.

But the Bible shows us not many pages later—and from the same pen as Ephesians—the good works of a woman and services that believers of either sex can provide. In 1 Timothy 5 we see that our good works include being faithful spouses, bringing up children, showing hospitality to strangers and fellow believers, and helping those in distress.

Good works are not a mystery that we have to meditate to find.

We just need to see the needs around us and meet them as God gives us the strength and resources to do so.

That's practical—and pure—Christianity.

Father, how often I have wondered about Your will for my life, thinking it was
something grand and glorious. But Your Word says it's all around me.
Help me to see and follow the good works that are within my reach.

HIS PERFECT STRENGTH

"My grace is sufficient for you, for my power is made perfect in weakness." Therefore I will boast all the more gladly about my weaknesses, so that Christ's power may rest on me.
2 CORINTHIANS 12:9 NIV

How do you define stress? Perhaps you feel it when the car doesn't start or the toilet backs up or the line is too long at the grocery store. Or maybe your source of stress is a terrible diagnosis, a late-night phone call, a demanding boss, or a broken relationship. It's probably a combination of all of these things. You might be able to cope with one of them, but when several are bearing down at once, stress is the inevitable result.

It has been said that stress results when our perceived demands exceed our perceived resources. When the hours required to meet a deadline at work (demand) exceed the number of hours we have available (resources), we get stressed. The most important word in this definition is *perceived*. When it comes to stress, people have a tendency to do two things. First, they magnify the demand ("I will *never* be able to get this done"), and second, they fail to consider all of their resources. For the children of God, this includes His mighty strength, which remains long after ours is gone.

In an uncertain world, not much can be said for sure. But no matter what life throws our way, we can be confident of this: our demands will *never* exceed God's vast resources.

Strong and mighty heavenly Father, thank You that in my weakness I can always rely on Your perfect strength. Amen.

WHY ME?

*I am Alpha and Omega, the beginning and the ending, saith the Lord,
which is, and which was, and which is to come, the Almighty.*
REVELATION 1:8 KJV

When we find ourselves in difficult situations, what do we do?

Many people look at those circumstances selfishly and cry, "Oh God, why me? Why do these things happen to *me*?"

But we mortals have a too-narrow view of our existence. In our minds, this world at this time is all there is. Sure, God is eternal—but maybe that just means He was around before us and had some foresight that we would come into being someday.

If that's our concept of God, we need to read His Word more closely.

Jesus said He is the "Alpha and Omega." He's the beginning and the end. Jesus, like the Father, *is*. He is the Ever-Present One who is apart from time.

When God spoke our world into existence, He called into being a certain reality, knowing then everything that ever was to happen—and everyone who ever was to be.

That you exist now is cause for rejoicing! God made *you* to fellowship with Him! If that fellowship demands trials for a season, rejoice that God thinks you worthy to share in the sufferings of Christ—and, eventually, in His glory.

Why do these things happen to you?

Because God in His infinite wisdom, love, and grace determined them to be. Praise His holy name!

*Father, I thank You for giving me this difficult time in my life.
Shine through all my trials today. I want You to get the glory.*

PEACE, BE STILL

GOD makes his people strong.
GOD gives his people peace.
PSALM 29:11 MSG

At the center of life's storms, how do we find peace? If we're tossed about, struggling and hopeless, where is the peace? Don't worry—peace can be ours for the asking.

You see, *God* is our peace. He is ready to calm our storms when we call on Him. He will comfort and strengthen us each day.

The Bible tells of Peter and the other disciples rowing their small boat against strong waves on the way to Capernaum. They knew Jesus was planning to join them, but they'd drifted out into the sea and left Him far behind. When they saw Jesus walking on the water, they were terrified—but He spoke and calmed their fears.

Impulsive Peter asked to meet Jesus on the water. He stepped out of the boat and, briefly, walked on the waves like his Lord. As long as Peter's eyes were on Jesus, he stayed atop the water—but the moment he looked away, he sank. Peter learned a valuable lesson.

The lesson works for believers today: Keep your eyes focused on the problems and you'll have mayhem. Focus on Jesus and you'll have peace.

Dear Lord, I thank You for Your protection.
Help me to keep my eyes on You. Please grant me peace.

IN HIS TIME

He has made everything beautiful in its time. He has also
set eternity in the human heart; yet no one can fathom
what God has done from beginning to end.
ECCLESIASTES 3:11 NIV

When we're in the midst of a struggle, it's difficult to picture how things could possibly end well. Maybe you're going through a situation where a happy ending looks impossible. But in spite of how things appear, God promises to make all things beautiful in His time.

That means there's a day coming when all of this hardship—the work, the hours spent caring for one in need, the pain—will be a priceless treasure to you. The memories will be precious.

It's good to remember that the Lord views everything in light of *eternity*. He isn't limited by time. So when He sees your life, He views it as a "forever" story. He knows that this season you're walking through—and it *is* a season—won't last forever. He also knows that one day you will look back on this time of life and view it as a gift.

Ask for God's perspective on this season, and thank Him for making it beautiful. . .in His time.

Dear Lord, please give me Your perspective. Help me to see that my
situation—tough as it is—will one day be a thing of great beauty to me.

SHE GAVE, AND HE GAVE BACK

Then Peter arose and went with them. When he was come, they brought him into the upper chamber: and all the widows stood by him weeping, and shewing the coats and garments which Dorcas made, while she was with them.
ACTS 9:39 KJV

Dorcas had spent her life as a servant. She was a follower of Christ who was "full of good works and almsdeeds" (Acts 9:36 KJV) that she did continually. Scripture does not itemize her works, but we do know that she sewed coats and garments and took care of many widows.

She was the type of woman who could have "worked herself to death." People like Dorcas are often so busy caring for others that they fail to care about themselves. Of course, we can't say that for sure about Dorcas.

But we definitely know that when she died, many people grieved. And when they heard that the apostle Peter was nearby, they asked him to come—apparently believing he could raise the dead.

That's exactly what Peter did. Through his prayer, he raised Dorcas and returned her to service.

Dorcas had given her life to serve God, and God had given it back.

"For whosoever will save his life shall lose it: and whosoever will lose his life for my sake shall find it" (Matthew 16:25 KJV).

When you give your life to serve others, you are honoring God—and finding life.

Lord Jesus, I don't understand why You would give Your life for me.
There is nothing greater that I can do on earth than to give my life for
You in service to others. Please strengthen me for this joyful task.

DON'T FORGET ME, LORD!

Think upon me, my God, for good,
according to all that I have done for this people.
NEHEMIAH 5:19 KJV

After the people of Judah lived for decades in exile, Nehemiah spent many busy years helping his people regroup. As governor of Judah, he helped rebuild Jerusalem's walls torn down by the Babylonians. It was an incredible feat that required every mental, physical, and spiritual resource Nehemiah could muster.

Nehemiah planned all the necessary stages of the work and figured out the finances with the Persian king, Artaxerxes. Although an aristocrat, Nehemiah labored alongside his people, doing the "heavy lifting" of the project. When enemies threatened to disrupt the work, Nehemiah turned "general," directing workers in military strategies. Even after the wall was completed, Nehemiah took responsibility for the people's spiritual welfare—contributions they did not always appreciate. He settled squabbles and even roughed up men who had foolishly married foreign wives. Exhausted after more than a decade of intense service, Nehemiah asked God to remember everything he had done for this needy group.

Nehemiah possessed excellent leadership abilities—but his faith in God proved to be the factor that pulled him through. When Nehemiah couldn't take it anymore, he ran to God.

Sometimes the sacrificial roles God asks us to assume last for days, months, even years. When no one seems to appreciate us, we, like Nehemiah, will find the support and affirmation we need in our heavenly Father.

Lord, when I feel I've poured my life out for nothing, please help me
care for others with Your heart. I thank You for Your faithful love.

EMBRACING CHANGE

May the Lord direct your hearts into
God's love and Christ's perseverance.
2 THESSALONIANS 3:5 NIV

Most people don't like change. Change can fill us with fear. It can take away our sense of security. Self-doubt and feelings of powerlessness can invade our mind and emotions. We want our old lives back—those days when we knew the rules. But in many situations, everything feels uncertain and unpredictable.

God has promised, though, to direct us through all the twists and turns of life. That guarantee should give us hope and strength. Knowing that, we can step away from our situation momentarily, take a deep breath, and proceed. Then, with the courage He offers, we can move forward on our new path. Even if our direction is unclear, we know we can take at least the first step. As we put one foot in front of the other, the path will eventually be revealed.

And God's love will continue to guide our steps along this new road.

Direct my way, Lord. Give me strength to embrace the changes in my life.
I don't see where I am going or how I will do this, but I know that
Your guidance and Christ's perseverance will lead my way.

GRAB HOLD OF HOPE

We. . .have every reason to grab the promised
hope with both hands and never let go.
HEBREWS 6:18 MSG

Martin Luther is quoted as saying, "Everything that is done in this world is done by hope."

God created us to hope—and then communicated hope to us in many different ways. The eternal hope we have in Christ is what keeps Christians moving forward rather than wallowing in self-pity. Caring for a dying loved one can rob us of hope unless we hang onto our hope of eternal life through Christ.

God promised that He would never leave us or forsake us. He gives strength to the weak. And to those who are brokenhearted, He promises comfort. Even on the darkest days, in the midst of the most difficult trials, His promises shine forth as beacons lighting our way. He is the same God who provided deliverance, protection, and comfort to His people, Israel.

Don't give up. Jesus died and rose again to give us an eternal hope. Rest in His promises today!

Lord, sometimes the days and nights are so long. I see no change in my loved one, or the change steals even more of life away. Yet You have promised to sustain me, to stay with me, to walk with me even through the valley of the shadow of death. Help me to keep my eyes on You and hold tightly to Your promises. Help me to never let go!

GOD'S STRENGTH

Be my strong refuge, to which I may resort continually; You have given the commandment to save me, for You are my rock and my fortress.
PSALM 71:3 NKJV

What in your life is completely zapping your strength? Whether it's relational, emotional, or physical (or all of the above), we all have issues in life that drag us down.

So where do we seek the strength we need? From an energy bar? A jolt of caffeine? A quick nap? Those things might supply energy, but energy is not strength. The strength we need is found in God alone.

God's strength is never generic. He knows where we hurt and what lies ahead for us, and the strength He provides matches up to our very personal needs.

When we wearily step out of bed, God is there to supply the physical strength we need to get us through the day. When bitter words are about to escape our mouths, He supplies the spiritual strength for us to stop and consider what we're about to say. When our feelings are raw, He gives the emotional strength we need to avoid weariness and hopelessness.

Let's go to God in our weakness and exchange it for His mighty strength. His strength has no end!

Gracious Father, You know how weak I can become. Thank You for supplying me with the strength to face all that will happen each day.

ANXIOUS ANTICIPATIONS

I am not saying this because I am in need, for I have
learned to be content whatever the circumstances.
PHILIPPIANS 4:11 NIV

Have you ever been so eager for the future that you forgot to be thankful for the present day?

We anxiously await the weekend, our next vacation, retirement, or some other future event. Maybe we're eager to start a new chapter in our life because we've been frustrated with our caretaking responsibilities.

Those of us who have raised children have felt a similar pull. We looked ahead to their first steps, their school days, their weddings. In all the daily responsibilities, we sometimes wished the kids would "just grow up." Then they did—and now we miss those little ones and their mischievous antics, wishing we could turn back the clock.

Humans have a tendency to complain about the problems and irritations of life. It's much less natural to appreciate the good things we have—until they're gone. While it's fine to look forward to the future, let's remember to reflect on all of *today's* blessings—the large and the small—and appreciate all that we do have.

Thank You, Lord, for the beauty of today. Please remind me when I
become preoccupied with the future and forget to enjoy the present.

....

....

....

....

....

....

....

....

ACCEPTABLE WORDS AND PLEASING THOUGHTS

May these words of my mouth and this meditation of my heart be
pleasing in your sight, LORD, my Rock and my Redeemer.
PSALM 19:14 NIV

We've all heard the saying, "Sticks and stones may break my bones, but words can never hurt me." Unfortunately, the latter portion of that saying isn't always true. Words *do* have the power to hurt others. In the Bible, James describes our tongues as very difficult to tame. Without God's help, it can't be done.

King David also knew the power of words. In Psalm 19 he praises God for revealing Himself in nature and through His Word. Verses 7–13 extol the wonders of God's Word and declare that it reveals not only God but also man's condition. David ends the psalm with a plea that his words, both spoken and unspoken, be acceptable and pleasing to God.

Often we're tempted to speak before we think—especially in times of stress and tiredness. Rather than bringing blessing to those around us, we might even curse those we love. We can rip into their weaknesses and tear down their character instead of lifting them up with encouragement.

Today, let's make David's prayer our own by meditating on the truth of God's Word. Then our words will truly be acceptable and pleasing—to the Lord and to our loved ones.

Father, please cleanse my mind of negative thoughts so that
the words I speak today are words of encouragement
and comfort to my loved ones as well as praise to You.

IS ANYONE LISTENING?

*And I will ask the Father, and He will give you another Comforter
(Counselor, Helper, Intercessor, Advocate, Strengthener, and Standby),
that He may remain with you forever.*
JOHN 14:16 AMPC

Christians have the assurance that God will hear them when they call. In turn, we can hear God's voice of love when *we* listen.

People who love each other spend time together. They share their dreams and hopes. So it is with our heavenly Father, who wants to hear from us. He cares so much that He sent the Holy Spirit to be our Counselor, our Comforter.

The Greek word for "comfort" is *paraklesis,* or "calling near." When we are called near to someone, we are able to hear his or her whisper. It is this very picture scripture paints when it speaks of the Holy Spirit. God sent the Spirit to whisper to us and to offer encouragement and guidance, to be our strength when all else fails. When we pray—when we tell God our needs and give Him praise—He listens. Then He directs the Spirit within us to speak to our hearts and give us reassurance.

Our world is filled with noise and distractions. Look for a place where you can be undisturbed for a few minutes. Take a deep breath, lift your prayers, and listen. God will speak—and your heart will hear.

*Dear Lord, I thank You for Your care.
Help me to recognize Your voice and to listen well.*

A FRESH PERSPECTIVE

*"Listen now to me and I will give you some advice,
and may God be with you."*
EXODUS 18:19 NIV

Moses was doing too much.

Exodus 18:2–3 tells us that the great leader of Israel sent away his wife, Zipporah, and their sons. Though the Bible doesn't elaborate, it appears that Moses was working too hard—possibly even neglecting his family. Maybe he sent them away because he couldn't work as hard as he was working and care for the family at the same time. Whatever the reason, his father-in-law, Jethro, decided to visit.

The next morning as usual, Moses got up to go to work. After observing Moses' exhausting routine, Jethro sat down with his son-in-law. "Why are you doing all the work yourself?" he asked. "You need to start delegating."

Moses was working so hard that he had lost his objectivity. Jethro provided him with a different—and helpful—perspective.

It's easy to get caught up in the "tyranny of the urgent" and lose perspective. When we take a step back and look at our lives more objectively, we often see alternative ways of doing things. Such insights can come from a trusted friend or relative.

What is there about your present situation that might require perspective from someone else? Is there something you could be doing differently? Is there a task you could be delegating or an option you haven't considered? Learn from Moses—take the advice of someone who could offer you a much-needed perspective.

*Heavenly Father, I thank You for the perspective that others can bring.
Teach me to listen to and heed wise advice.*

UNCHAINED!

*The Spirit you received does not make you slaves, so that you live
in fear again; rather, the Spirit you received brought about
your adoption to sonship. And by him we cry, "Abba, Father."*
ROMANS 8:15 NIV

Imagine how difficult life would be inside prison walls. No sunlight. No freedom to go where you wanted when you wanted. Just a dreary, dark existence, locked away in a place you did not choose, with no way of escape.

Most of us can't even imagine such restrictions. As Christians we have complete freedom through Jesus Christ, our Lord and Savior. No limitations. No chains.

Ironically, many of us build our own walls and choose our own chains. When we give ourselves over to fear, we're deliberately entering a prison the Lord never intended for us. We don't always do it willfully. In fact, we often find ourselves behind bars after the fact, then wonder how we got there.

Do you struggle with fear? Do you feel it binding you with its invisible chains? If so, then there's good news. Through Jesus, you have received the Spirit of sonship. A son (or daughter) of the most high God has nothing to fear. Knowing you've been set free is enough to make you cry, "Abba, Father!" in praise. Today, acknowledge your fears to the Lord. He will loose your chains and set you free.

*Lord, thank You that You are the great chain-breaker! I don't have to live in fear.
I am Your child, Your daughter, and You are my Daddy-God!*

LEADING THE WAY

The LORD himself goes before you and will be with you; he will never leave you nor forsake you. Do not be afraid; do not be discouraged.
DEUTERONOMY 31:8 NIV

Does life sometimes feel like a walk in a dense fog?

Fog prevents us from seeing what lies ahead—just as our fears and worries can. Will we be able to handle the stress or make the right decisions? Will people offer to help us? Will the boss understand if we aren't able to make it to work? There are so many unknowns—and when we can't see beyond our present situations, it's easy to feel lost.

Whatever our struggles, we have Someone who sees our paths clearly. God's Word says that He goes ahead of us. The first step on this path isn't really ours because God Himself has already taken it. He can lead us through whatever lies ahead because He knows the way.

There is no better guide or companion for life's journey than our all-knowing heavenly Father.

Dear Lord, thank You for going ahead of me. Thank You also for being ever present with me. With You having paved my way, I can walk in confidence, not fear.

FIRST THINGS FIRST

Get up and eat, for the journey is too much for you.
1 KINGS 19:7 NIV

Elijah's work had dragged him down physically. One time, he was so exhausted that he begged God to take his life.

It's interesting to note what God *didn't* do for Elijah in response to that prayer: God didn't kill Elijah, nor did He say, "Stop your whining and get back to work." The first thing God did was send an angel to attend to Elijah's physical needs. In His wisdom, God knew that Elijah wouldn't see his situation clearly until he was nourished and well rested.

When the demands of our lives become too much, it's tempting to stop right where we are and beg God to release us from our circumstances. And on those days, the best prescription may well be a nourishing meal or a good night's sleep. It's amazing what those things can do to revive our souls.

As women, caring for our own physical needs should be high on our priority list. Are there extra things in the schedule we can eliminate so we can get more sleep? Would a little planning allow us to eat more healthily?

Ask God for wisdom to evaluate your lifestyle and, if necessary, plan the steps you should take to sustain your physical well-being. It may take some up-front effort, but the dividends will be well worth it.

Father, I thank You for the relief You provide when the journey is too much for me. Teach me to eat well and get enough rest and to care for this physical body You've given me.

DID GOD SAY. . . ?

For we walk by faith, not by sight.
2 Corinthians 5:7 nasb

The more complex life becomes, the easier it is to lose perspective.

Maybe we begin to feel overwhelmed with everything we are responsible for. There must be someone else who can do a better job, who can handle all the stuff that comes up, who can do it more graciously than we can. Did God really say *we* should do this?

This is the time faith really comes into play. God *has* given us the task—and we must believe that not only has He asked us to do this job, but He's also given us an abundance of mental, emotional, and physical supply. And not just once, but over and over every morning.

Rarely can we see our way clearly, but we can believe that God has the situation under His perfect control. We can believe that He will work it for His glory and for the good of ourselves and those around us.

As we learn to become more and more dependent on God, we trust Him more and more. Our faith, though it may have begun the size of a mustard seed, will grow into a mighty tree.

Lord, I thank You for choosing me to work with You. Give me the faith I need to see Your hand in everyday circumstances and to ask You for the help I need.

LIFE PRESERVERS

My comfort in my suffering is this:
your promise preserves my life.
PSALM 119:50 NIV

It's the law for boaters in many states: always wear your life preserver. The purpose is simple. A life preserver keeps people afloat—and their heads above water—should they accidentally fall overboard. The device's buoyancy can even keep an unconscious person afloat in a face-up position as long as it's worn properly.

God is our life preserver in this life. When we are battered by the waves of trouble, we can expect God to understand and to comfort us in our distress. His Word, like a buoyant life preserver, holds us up in the bad times.

But the life preserver only works if you put it on *before* your boat sinks. To get into God's life jacket, put your arms into the sleeves of prayer and tie the vest with biblical words. God will surround you with His love and protection—even if you're unconscious of His presence. He promises to keep our heads above water in the storms of life.

Preserving God, I cling to You as my life preserver. Keep my head
above the turbulent water of life so I don't drown. Bring me safely to the shore.

WITNESSES

*Therefore, since we are surrounded by such a great cloud of witnesses,
let us throw off everything that hinders and the sin that so easily entangles.
And let us run with perseverance the race marked out for us.*
HEBREWS 12:1 NIV

A few days before she died, a godly woman was granted a view into heaven. When asked what she saw, she said, "People. Lots of people."

When asked what they were doing, she replied, "They are waiting to welcome me."

"Who are they?" was the next question. The woman started telling of family members who had gone on before. Then she named several whom she'd led to the Lord during her lifetime. Before long she stopped, tired of talking and awed by the number of people who were awaiting her arrival.

This story reminds us of the "great cloud of witnesses" a Bible writer describes in Hebrews 11 and 12. It's so easy for us to feel unnoticed, unappreciated, even forgotten by our friends, family, and fellow church members. We forget that we have an invisible crowd of believers who have gone on before us, many of whom suffered persecution and horrible deaths for doing right, for staying faithful to the tasks the Lord had given them to do. They are encouraging us to keep on, to throw aside everything that weighs us down and keeps us from running the race marked out for us.

Father, help me to remember that I am not alone in this task. Many have gone on before me, leaving an example of faithful service. May I one day hear You say, "Well done, good and faithful servant!" (Matthew 25:21 NIV).

LAYING DOWN YOUR LIFE

Greater love hath no man than this,
that a man lay down his life for his friends.
JOHN 15:13 KJV

God-breathed love is sacrificial. It continues to give even under the most difficult of circumstances, never keeping track of the cost. As indicated in today's scripture, the ultimate expression of love is one's willingness to lay down one's own life for another.

We wonder if such love is really possible—and if we have it in ourselves to love so sacrificially. Does this scripture refer only to literal death, or is there a deeper message?

Sacrifice, by its very definition, is the ability to place another's needs before your own—to continue pouring out even when you're tapped out. Every instance you give of your time, energy, or resources to care for a loved one in need, you demonstrate your willingness to lay down your life. You're expressing the heart of God.

Your ability to continue giving day in and day out pleases the heart of your heavenly Father, who perfectly understands the principle of "laying down" one's life. After all, that's what He did for us at Calvary.

Dear Lord, please create Your heart within me—a heart ready to give
sacrificially no matter the cost. When I feel I'm "given out,"
remind me of Your great sacrifice on the cross for me.

CONSTANT PRAYER

Be unceasing in prayer.
1 THESSALONIANS 5:17 AMPC

Paul's statement concerning prayer seems impossible. Nonstop prayer? How can we ever achieve that in our hectic world?

By our awareness of God. Through it, we become conscious of Him and discern His active involvement in our lives. God wants to have a relationship with us, and prayer demonstrates our faith in Him. His Word tells us to stay in constant contact.

Nineteenth-century preacher Charles Spurgeon described the Christian's prayer life as follows: "Like the old knights, always in warfare, not always on their steeds dashing forward with their lances raised to unhorse an adversary, but always wearing their weapons where they could readily reach them. . . . Those grim warriors often slept in their armor; so even when we sleep, we are still to be in the spirit of prayer, so that if perchance we wake in the night we may still be with God."

Prayer strengthens us for any battle. It's our armor and our mightiest weapon against fear, doubt, discouragement, and worry. Prayer changes our perspective and allows us to face the cares of each day. When our whole world is falling apart, prayer can keep us together.

That's why constant prayer is so important.

Dear Father, I want to be in the center of Your will.
Please help me to "be unceasing in prayer."

THE POWER OF GRATITUDE

It is a good thing to give thanks unto the Lord.
PSALM 92:1 KJV

Gloria's friends often feel sorry for her—she provides seemingly tireless care for her ailing husband and doesn't have time for outings or special events. But when her friends ask her about it, Gloria tells them, "I don't have time to feel sorry for myself. I have too much for which to be thankful!"

"Being thankful" doesn't mean we live in denial of our problems—nor does it minimize the fact that life can sometimes be very hard. But God's Word does tell us to give thanks—in all circumstances. Gloria knows that the purpose of gratefulness is transformational. It gives us perspective on our situations, keeps us from feeling sorry for ourselves, teaches us to rely on God, and reminds us that all we have comes from Him.

Hardships help us to grow. Even when we feel we have nothing else for which to give thanks, we can be grateful that God loves us enough to want to make us more like Him.

Let's take a moment today to count our blessings. We may find we're so busy being grateful that we won't have time to feel bad.

Father, I thank You for the ways that You reveal yourself to me.
Thank You for the many blessings You have given me and
that I can always think of something for which to be grateful.

IN STEP

Since we live by the Spirit,
let us keep in step with the Spirit.
GALATIANS 5:25 NIV

Early one morning, members of a traveling family stopped at a rest area. After eight more hours of driving in a hot, cramped car, they stopped to stretch their legs at a very similar-looking rest area. One of the young boys exclaimed, "I know this place. This is where we ate breakfast!"

"Oh, I hope not," muttered the travel-weary mom. But as she looked around, she could understand how her son had reached that conclusion. Everything—the buildings, the landscaping, the picnic tables—looked the same.

Sometimes we see our lives like that young boy perceived the roadside rest area. We spend time and effort completing all those routine tasks—but when we take stock, we conclude that we aren't getting anywhere. Like the weary mom, we hoped that our efforts would always propel us toward our destination.

Good news: the mom had read the map and road signs and knew she and her family were *not* where they had started. They hadn't just been spinning their wheels.

By reading our map (the Bible) and the signs (God's Spirit speaking to our hearts), we can know that we, too, are moving in the right direction.

It might not look like it. We might not get to our ultimate destination quickly. But we *will* get there—in God's time and in His way. Just keep in step with His Spirit!

Lord, as I complete my routine, help me to keep in step with Your Spirit.
You know where I'm headed, and You will get me there on time.

RENEWABLE SOURCE OF ENERGY

To this end I strenuously contend with all the energy
Christ so powerfully works in me.
COLOSSIANS 1:29 NIV

Wind, sun, water, and geothermal heat are all examples of renewable energy sources. These abundant and powerful assets supply our power needs to fuel our homes and businesses.

As women, we also need energy to complete our tasks. Our daily labor drains our strength when we try to complete our work solely in our own power. A lack of energy can be a symptom of trying to do too much on our own rather than relying on God. Think of it this way: Have you ever tried to move furniture by yourself? When others help out, we draw on their energy and power to share the load.

When our energy runs low, where can we turn for renewal? To God. But before doing so, we must admit that we are trying to work all by ourselves. We must also recognize that negative emotions like anger and disappointment sap our energy.

When we then take stock of ourselves and ask God for help, He promises us access to His unlimited source of energy. His bottomless supply is ready for tapping. All we need to do is plug into His power by pausing in His presence, soaking up His love and comfort.

God will sustain us in our struggles when we refuel by praying, reading His Word, and basking in His presence. His energy works within us as an abundant and powerful asset to renew our strength.

Energetic Father, work within me with Your renewable power.
Thank You for being my source of strength and energy.
Your power is abundant and knows no limits.

MISSING THE MERCY IN THE MAYHEM

For the Lord will not cast off for ever: but though he cause grief,
yet will he have compassion according to the multitude of his mercies.
LAMENTATIONS 3:31–32 KJV

The days are too busy. The nights, too long. The pain, too great. The sorrow, too overwhelming.

And yet, somehow, you go on caring for those the Lord has put in your life.

How is this possible?

It comes through the infinite, renewable mercy of God. Every new morning comes with new mercy.

Sometimes, though, we miss the mercy in the mayhem. Because we tend to be brilliant multitaskers, we can easily reduce life to a set of activities and errands that we think we can control.

As we move from one task to the next, we may start thinking that we are managing things pretty well by ourselves—and we might fail to see the hand of God in our lives.

Let's slow down, step back, and look at the bigger picture. We can do nothing apart from God's mercy. Let's acknowledge His hand on our lives and stop trusting our own strength.

If we're managing at all, it's because God is upholding us, bearing our burdens, and sustaining us with His compassion and grace.

Father, how often I think I'm managing life well on my own. But I couldn't care for these people without Your help. I thank You for Your compassion and mercy each day. Without You, I could do nothing.

ARM IN ARM

The LORD is my strength and my defense; he has become my salvation.
He is my God, and I will praise him.
EXODUS 15:2 NIV

Accompanied by his son, an older gentleman began his daily walk. Side by side, the two strolled down the sidewalk, the son adjusting his steps to match his dad's. When they approached a crossroad, the older man turned toward an incline. His son suggested the level grade. Shaking his head, the gentleman said, "Walking uphill strengthens me." The son took his father's elbow, and they began to climb.

How often we turn to level ground and try to avoid the hills. Yet it's the hard path that strengthens us. Through our difficult times, God draws near and takes us by the arm. He becomes our guide and companion—and strength.

Moses and the children of Israel faced undeniable peril. With warriors behind and the Red Sea before, where could they turn? In the nick of time, God saved them by parting the waters. Shadrach, Meshach, and Abednego stepped into the fiery furnace, believing that God would rescue them. He didn't let them down.

Whatever we face, God is bigger than the circumstances. With God, all things are possible. Choose today to believe that He will move in a mighty way. Choose today to cling to His arm and walk up the mountainside.

Dear Father, help me to learn to depend on You daily.
Show me Your mercy and grace, I pray.

A FRAGRANT OFFERING

Follow God's example, therefore, as dearly loved children and walk in the way of love, just as Christ loved us and gave himself up for us as a fragrant offering and sacrifice to God.

EPHESIANS 5:1–2 NIV

Have you ever walked into a place that smelled beautiful? Scented candles, potpourri, or fresh cookies in the oven can be very inviting, drawing us in and making us want to stay for a while.

In a similar way, if we carry the scent of Christ in our daily walk, people will be drawn to us and want to "stay for a while." But how do we give off that amazing, inviting fragrance?

There's really only one way—by imitating God. By patterning our actions after His. By loving others fully. By seeing them through His eyes. By looking with great compassion on those who are hurting, as Jesus did when He went about healing the sick and pouring out His life for those in need.

As we live a life of love in front of those we care for, we exude the sweetest fragrance of all—Christ. That's one aroma that can't be bottled!

Dear Lord, I long to live a life that points people to You. As I care for those in need, may the sweet-smelling aroma of You and Your love be an invitation for people to draw near.

BEANS OR STEAK?

Each of you must bring a gift in proportion
to the way the LORD your God has blessed you.
DEUTERONOMY 16:17 NIV

At the harvest celebration, every Jew was to thank God with a sacrifice according to the blessings He'd given. God's Word assumes that every believer would receive a blessing of some sort. At the very least, His people were alive because He provided food for them. Those who didn't have much more than that would bring a small but heartfelt offering. Others, blessed with physical abundance, brought a generous offering of much greater value.

Our blessings may not be the kind we'd like: we may look for extra money to pay off bills, while God sends us spiritual strength. But just as God provided for His Old Testament people even in the years of lean harvests, He provides for us.

We may be eating more beans and rice than steak and lobster, but isn't the former better for us in the long run? While we're looking for the good life, God's looking at what's good for us. Sometimes that means physical blessing—but other times it's a spiritual challenge.

No matter what our circumstances, God is blessing us—if we're following Him with steadfastness. Let's bless Him in return with our thanksgiving.

Lord, I thank You for the many blessings You give.
In exchange, I offer You the gift of my heart and life.

DOES ANYONE HEAR?

And it shall come to pass, that before they call, I will answer;
and while they are yet speaking, I will hear.
ISAIAH 65:24 KJV

Pam hurried out the kitchen door with her to-do list clenched between her teeth. As she slid behind the wheel of her car, she wondered how she could accomplish everything. With an eight-to-five job on weekdays, Saturday was supposed to be less structured—a time for laundry, housekeeping, groceries, and maybe, just maybe, a little time for fun. *Fun?* Pam had almost forgotten that word.

Pam's cell phone interrupted her thoughts. *What now?* She sighed.

"Mom," her seventeen-year-old daughter said, "could you pick up that book on hold at the library for me? And don't worry about dinner—I'm making the Crock-Pot recipe we talked about yesterday. Stay as long as you need, and give Gram a hug, okay?"

Pam smiled as she pulled into the nursing home parking lot. She and her mom could have an unhurried visit now. In fact, with dinner taken care of, she just might have a few minutes for some fun at the mall.

It's true. Sometimes God does answer before we call!

Dear God, You are the perfect Father, seeing and meeting my every need.
Thank You for providing rest, relief, and recreation.

CONTAGIOUS HOPE

[Jesus] died for us, a death that triggered life. Whether we're awake with the living or asleep with the dead, we're alive with him! So speak encouraging words to one another. Build up hope so you'll all be together in this, no one left out, no one left behind. I know you're already doing this; just keep on doing it.

1 THESSALONIANS 5:10–11 MSG

What do we have to lose? Alive here on earth or dancing on heaven's streets of gold, we have life with Jesus. Do you see the power of that? When we can wrap our hearts and minds around that concept, we can make a real difference for others. Fleshed out, this hope provides a contagious encouragement that warms others with its radiance.

We are in a position to give that hope to others in great need. Our well-placed words of encouragement can build up our loved ones, transferring the Life that's within us to their hungry hearts. In a world often narrowed by confinement or pain, their positive perspectives can dwindle—so they need our wider vision of abundant life in Christ.

Bring them along on this joyful journey. Smile, look them square in the eyes, and speak the truth of God's love to them. As we minister daily to their needs, we build them up in ways that no one else could possibly do.

Father, please give me specific words of encouragement for those I serve today. May the hope within me be contagious, infecting them with Your abundant life.

CREATE A FESTIVE ATMOSPHERE

A joyful heart is good medicine,
but a broken spirit dries up the bones.
PROVERBS 17:22 NASB

Loneliness—it can creep up on us, even when we're busy caring for our loved ones.

Haven't we all felt the burden of isolation at one time or another? But we don't have to stay in that lonely place. Sometimes even a minor change in our routine can lift our spirits and the spirit of our loved one. With just a little effort, ordinary days can become extraordinary.

Lighting a candle can brighten the gloomiest of days. The aroma of an apple pie or chocolate-chip cookies baking has a comforting effect. We might play some pleasant background music or pop a lighthearted comedy into the DVD player.

Lonely days are perfect for inviting friends or neighbors over for an impromptu visit. It's fun to hear about the unusual experiences of our friends' lives—invite them to share stories of their childhoods, describe some of the most funny people they've met, or tell about their most embarrassing moments. Such get-togethers are often sprinkled with humor and surprises.

God knows that a joyful heart is good medicine, helping both us and our loved ones to feel better.

Dear Lord, sometimes I feel lonely. I need Your touch.
Thank You for filling the void in my heart with Your joy.

WHEN GOD RENOVATES

God is the builder of everything.
HEBREWS 3:4 NIV

While planning to renovate the living room, a husband and wife most wanted to change two large rectangular posts that stood floor-to-ceiling in the middle of the room.

But the couple's cautious contractor didn't remove the posts. He explained that, without the posts as support, the room's ceiling could come crashing down.

Unlike that contractor, God—the renovator of hearts—doesn't work cautiously. When He begins renovations, He removes (or allows the removal of) all existing supports. Maybe one such "support" is health—ours or a loved one's. Maybe it's our savings. Maybe it's something else. Our lives, as we know them, crash. We hurt. We don't know how we can go on.

But God knows. If we let Him, He'll replace the temporary supports we'd relied on—health, independence, ability, you name it—with eternal spiritual supports like faith, surrender, and prayer. Those supports enable us to live lives of true freedom abounding with spiritual blessing.

Lord, I am tempted to cling to the supports I've erected.
When my life crashes, I'm tempted to despair. Please help me to
be still and place my trust in You, the great builder of all lives.

WHAT WE SEE IS NOT WHAT WE GET

*God. . .gives life to the dead and calls those
things which do not exist as though they did.*
ROMANS 4:17 NKJV

Disaster after disaster overwhelms us: Our loved one's health deteriorates. Medical bills pile up. Insurance balks at paying. Our spirits plummet.

Then the car won't start.

The circumstances of life seem to crash in on us like enormous waves over a small fishing boat. We feel like Jesus' doused disciples on the stormy Sea of Galilee—deserted by a sleeping Lord.

We desperately scamper to solve our own problems. We try to keep our heads above water on the tumultuous sea of life. We pray like the frantic disciples prayed: "Lord, don't you care that we are perishing?"

Or we say—like Martha did after her brother, Lazarus, died—"Lord, if You were here, things wouldn't be like this."

God understands our perspective. Sure, the circumstances look bad. But He's the God who asks us to exercise faith. With faith, what we see is *not* what we get. With faith we get *God*—His company and every spiritual blessing.

Stop looking at circumstances. Start looking at God. He is in control. Have faith!

*Lord, please grow faith in my heart so that I will know with certainty that
You are in charge—that You are arranging my circumstances for my
good and Your glory. Let me be fully convinced—like Abraham was—
that You are able and willing to keep Your promises to me.*

QUIET HOPE

It's a good thing to quietly hope,
quietly hope for help from GOD.
LAMENTATIONS 3:26 MSG

Hope is essential to life. Without it, life has no meaning, no purpose.

How much truer that is in our spiritual lives. The hope of eternal life in heaven grows more powerful the longer we live in our earthly bodies. Hope keeps us going in the midst of trouble and heartache. It allows us to live in expectation of life with no pain, no sorrow, no trouble of any kind to mar our eternal existence.

Jeremiah is often called the "weeping prophet." Yet even in his lament over Judah's sin and turning away from God, he wrote these words: "It's a good thing to quietly hope. . .for help from God." Dwelling on the confusion and chaos of his day only added to Jeremiah's distress. The prophet knew that keeping his focus on the Lord was essential to seeing the hope of his people's salvation, which God had promised.

God calls us to "cease striving" (Psalm 46:10 NASB) so that we can know Him and understand the hope of His calling (Ephesians 1:18). He wants us to quietly hope and wait on God's promises for strength (Isaiah 40:31), for endurance (1 Corinthians 10:13), for peace (Romans 15:13), for salvation (1 Thessalonians 5:8), for eternal life in heaven (Titus 1:2)—for others as well as for ourselves.

Lord, help me to be quiet before You today no matter what is going on around me. I look to the hope I have in Christ Jesus for all I need to do Your will today.

TAKE TIME TO SIT

*And Jesus answered and said unto her, Martha, Martha, thou art careful
and troubled about many things: but one thing is needful: and Mary
hath chosen that good part, which shall not be taken away from her.*
LUKE 10:41–42 KJV

Martha, the busy sister of the devoted Mary, has had a lot of bad press over the
centuries. "Don't be a Martha," we're told. "Be a Mary."

But while she's often criticized, Martha had many good qualities. She was a dili-
gent worker. She was a natural leader with a passion for serving.

The problem is that Martha didn't take time to sit. And because she didn't, she
missed out on a deeper relationship with the One she served.

As we serve others, it's so easy to be on the run. But we must take time to sit. Certainly, we want to sit at the Lord's feet, to be quiet before Him. But we should also sit
with those we serve.

Sitting gives us a chance to breathe—and to gain perspective. It gives us time to
develop relationships with those we serve.

When the toddler decorates the bedroom with baby powder, clean it up, hug him,
and thank God for his energy. Then play a game with him—even if you don't have
time.

After cleaning up a bedridden parent, sit by his side, hold his hand, and talk.

The goodness of these times—the love, respect, and joy—will never be taken away.

Father, I am drained from being on the run.
Help me to sit more, both with those I serve and with You.

....

....

....

....

....

....

....

BUILDING TRUST

Trust in the LORD with all your heart and lean not on your own understanding;
in all your ways submit to him, and he will make your paths straight.
PROVERBS 3:5–6 NIV

Many corporations send their employees to leadership training courses in the hope that they will develop better working relationships. One exercise takes place on a rope course. A person is buckled into a harness on a high platform, then falls into open space, trusting team members to guide him safely back to the ground.

If we can trust people with our lives while dangling in midair, why is it so difficult to put our trust in a loving heavenly Father? Perhaps it's because we can't see God. Trust—what some call "blind faith"—is not easily attained. It comes after we've built a record with others over time.

To trust God, we have to step out in faith. The adage "Let go and let God" sounds simple. It isn't—but it works. Try this: challenge yourself to trust God with one detail in your life each day. Build that trust pattern and watch Him work.

He won't let you down. He holds you securely in His hand. He is your hope for the future.

Dear Father, I want to rely on You. Help me learn to trust You this day.

DISCERNING HEARTS

I am your servant; give me discernment
that I may understand your statutes.
PSALM 119:125 NIV

Discernment is the ability to listen for God's guidance and wisdom when making decisions. As Christians, this is one of our most valuable tools—and one of our most important prayers should be, "Give me discernment, Lord."

We are bombarded by important questions that deserve thoughtful answers. Our decisions affect many people, both now and in the future. Which of the overwhelming issues should we address first? Who needs to be involved with those decisions? What are the financial ramifications? How do we find the answers to these problems?

We pray for wisdom. We involve others in the process by consulting with family, friends, and professionals. We explore our options by getting all the information available to us, and we simply give the process time. Ultimately, we let it rest in God's hands.

Then we remember to be gentle with ourselves over the situations that don't turn out as we had hoped. None of us is perfect—but if we listen for God's wisdom, we'll find the answers we need.

Guiding Father, You know what is best at every crossroad of decision.
As Your servant, I ask for Your guidance and wisdom.
Please give me the discernment I need.

FAITHFUL GOD

He who calls you is faithful, who also will do it.
1 THESSALONIANS 5:24 NKJV

When Moses encountered God in the burning bush, he wasn't thrilled with the assignment God had for him: to go to Pharaoh and seek the freedom of the Israelites.

Moses posed several questions to God in Exodus 3 and 4: "Who am I to go before Pharaoh?" "Who shall I tell the people of Israel sent me?" "What if they don't believe me?" "Why me, since I am slow of speech and slow of tongue?"

The Lord patiently reminded Moses that He would always be with him—that Moses wouldn't have to face Pharaoh alone. God told Moses His name: the great I AM, the God of Moses' ancestors. Then God equipped Moses with special signs to prove that he had been sent of the Lord. When Moses raised his last objection, God reminded him that He had made Moses' mouth and given him everything he needed to accomplish the task at hand. God was never angry with Moses until Moses said, in effect, "God, this sounds wonderful, but I'm not the man for the job. Find someone else."

Have you been called to a job you feel totally inadequate to accomplish? That's okay. God is faithful to fulfill His calling for you. All He wants are willing vessels.

Father, I thank You that You always equip us to do the work
You have called us to do. Help us to go forth in Your strength today.

UNRESPONSIVE? MAYBE NOT

*He said: "In my distress I called to the L*ORD*, and he answered me.*
From deep in the realm of the dead I called for help, and you listened to my cry."
JONAH 2:2 NIV

In the hallway of the nursing home, Amy sat beside Kate, who slumped sideways in her wheelchair.

"Your hair looks nice today," Amy began. No response.

"Can you hear the music? That is one of your favorite songs." Silence.

"I have a funny story to tell you. . ." Still no response.

Amy looked around in embarrassment to see if anyone was watching the one-way conversation.

Kate no longer recognized Amy's voice, said her name, or squeezed her hand. Most of the time Kate's eyes were shut. Even when they opened, a bland, dull stare was all that was visible.

What's the use? Amy thought. *I can't get through to her anymore.*

Discouraged, Amy ended the visit in her usual manner, reciting the Lord's Prayer. Holding Kate's hand, Amy whispered, "Our Father, who art in heaven. . ."

Surprisingly, Kate's weak voice continued, "Hallowed be thy name. . ."

With tears streaming down her cheeks, Amy thought, *I can't get through to you anymore—but God can.*

Lord, we call and You answer us. You never forget us when
we cry out to You, even in the silent prayers of our hearts.

MARTYR OR SERVANT?

Let nothing be done through strife or vainglory; but in lowliness
of mind let each esteem other better than themselves.
PHILIPPIANS 2:3 KJV

As we minister to those around us, we must constantly be on guard against the flesh.

While our spirit delights in serving, sometimes our flesh fights against it. We can easily slip from humility to pride, from being servants to thinking ourselves martyrs:

"Why must I always be the one to do this? Why can't anyone else help?"

"Where is this person's family, Lord? Why aren't they helping?"

"Go on without me—I'll just stay here alone *again* with Grandma."

Let's be vigilant to keep the selfish martyr's complex from putting down roots in our hearts. It leads only to bitterness and resentment.

The antidote, of course, is to remember the example of Jesus and allow the Spirit to put His mind in us.

"Let this mind be in you, which was also in Christ Jesus: who. . .made himself of no reputation, and took upon him the form of a servant, and was made in the likeness of men: and being found in fashion as a man, he humbled himself, and became obedient unto death, even the death of the cross" (Philippians 2:5–8 KJV).

Let us always serve as Christ served: for the benefit of others.

Father, I have not served to the point of blood as Jesus did. Nothing I can do
will ever come close. Strike down my pride, and let me always
minister with a humble and cheerful heart.

PASSWORD, PLEASE

Now if we are children, then we are heirs—heirs of God and co-heirs with Christ,
if indeed we share in his sufferings in order that we may also share in his glory.
ROMANS 8:17 NIV

Passwords are required everywhere, it seems: ATM machines, computer settings, bill paying. Passwords identify the user. They are intended to keep others out of our business. We're urged to change them frequently to protect our identity.

Christians have but one password: *Jesus.* Once we acquire this password through salvation, we become heirs of God with Him. We're children of the king. Precious saints. The Father gives us His own name to set us apart from the world.

Unlike computer or ATM passwords, this special name can never be compromised. We are safe and secure in the Father's arms, able to access every gift promised. Read the scriptures to see all that is available to you as a believer: eternal life, provision, promise after promise, blessing upon blessing.

Do you have your password, ready to swing open the gates of heaven? It's *Jesus.* Jesus, *period.* No other name is needed—no other combination.

You can take that to the bank.

Dear heavenly Father, today I choose to follow You.
I give You my life, my all. Teach me Your ways, and guard my heart.

GIVE IT ALL

Jesus looked him hard in the eye—and loved him! He said, "There's one thing left: Go sell whatever you own and give it to the poor. All your wealth will then be heavenly wealth. And come follow me." The man's face clouded over. This was the last thing he expected to hear, and he walked off with a heavy heart. He was holding on tight to a lot of things, and not about to let go.

MARK 10:21–22 MSG

It wasn't the response the rich young ruler wanted to hear. Things usually went his way. His position and prestige afforded him that.

But these straightforward, piercing words, blended with the love in Jesus' eyes, troubled the man's soul. It just was too much. He understood just what was being asked of him—everything! The pain in his heart was reflected on his face and in his posture as he slumped away. The truth was, this ruler was not ready to relinquish his all for Jesus.

What has Christ asked *you* to let go of? To what are you holding tightly? Most of us don't have great wealth (we might wish for that kind of "problem"), but are we willing to give up what we *do* have to serve Him?

Outwardly, we may look fine. But inwardly? Are our motives pure? Do we have an "underground" thought life? Is there anger bubbling beneath our calm surface?

The stresses of life can bring such trouble spots to light in our lives. Today let's face the truth of exactly who we are and give up those things that prevent us from wholeheartedly serving Jesus.

Lord, show me what I need to relinquish to You. Help me to abandon everything to freely and joyfully serve You.

SEEING THE LIGHT

"I am the light of the world."
JOHN 9:5 NKJV

Let's be honest with ourselves. We've all faced those "dark" moments that life can bring. We've experienced bouts of self-pity, frustration, anger, envy, doubt, confusion, even despair.

Like people deep within a cave, we've found ourselves surrounded by a blackness that seems overwhelming. Doubts assail us. We question ourselves and the decisions we're making. We may even doubt God's concern for us, wondering if He's totally unaware of how badly we hurt.

Jesus doesn't want this darkness to swallow us. Have you ever noticed the light that a full moon gives off? Far more powerful than that is Jesus' light. It cuts through the darkness, sending it fleeing away. His light shows us the path we should travel, a path filled with encouragement and hope.

Don't stumble around in the darkness of despair. When gloom and shadows try to overtake you, call on Jesus. The darkness is no match for His true light.

Dear God, it's easy to get caught up in discouraging thoughts or feelings of helplessness. May I see Your light in all my situations—and may it guide me safely home.

CEASE STRIVING

"Cease striving and know that I am God."
PSALM 46:10 NASB

In the midst of trouble and the chaos of daily living, our souls cry out for quiet, for peace, for calm. We are weak, pulled in every direction by our responsibilities and by the expectations of others. Often we forget that there is great power in *quiet*. In fact, our souls demand a zone of silence. Our God calls us to cease striving against all that would distract us from Him, to be still and learn to depend on Him to straighten out the tangles of our lives.

Many of the churches of post-Reformation Germany lapsed into ritualism after the vibrant change that had characterized the reformers. To counteract this, the Pietist Movement emphasized the need of being quiet before God in order to experience His peace. One of the more popular hymns to come from that movement emphasized the reality of the Christian life versus external show. According to Katharina von Schlegel, the writer of "Be Still, My Soul," recognizing who God is and what He can do goes a long way toward calming our inner spirits:

Be still, my soul: thy God doth undertake
To guide the future, as He has the past.
Thy hope, thy confidence let nothing shake;
All now mysterious shall be bright at last.
Be still, my soul: the waves and winds still know
His voice who ruled them while He dwelt below.

Father, You desire the best for me. Today may I cease striving against
the trouble and turmoil and allow You to guide my future as You have my past.

GOD—OUR CONSTANT COMPANION

When I remember You on my bed, I meditate on You in the night watches,
for You have been my help, and in the shadow of Your wings I sing for joy.
My soul clings to You; Your right hand upholds me.
PSALM 63:6–8 NASB

Worry. All too often, it robs us of precious sleep. The future is uncertain. Finances trouble us, especially when those big, unexpected costs pop up. Sometimes it's hard to release our troubles to the Lord. It's hard just to relax.

If you find you can't sleep, make good use of that wakeful time in the night hours—talk to God about your fears. He hears every prayer of His needy children, and He fills them with His peace.

Sometimes it helps to write our problems on paper and set them aside to deal with in the morning. God may surprise us with creative ideas while we sleep, showing us His divine way to handle our concerns.

Worried chicks, fearful of the world around them, run to their mother hen, who lifts her wings to protect her little ones. In the same way, God invites us to hide under His wings. There we find shelter and joy, knowing that we're never alone.

Thank You, Lord, for helping me release my burdens and trust
You for the outcome. Help me to get a good night's sleep
so that I can feel strong and well during the day.

HE IS YOUR CONFIDENCE

For the LORD will be your confidence,
and will keep your foot from being caught.
PROVERBS 3:26 NKJV

Sometimes we wish for more confidence. A job interview or a social situation we are facing may make us nervous. A new situation we're thrown into may cause us to worry. Will we be dressed appropriately? Will we know what to say?

Those are the times to remember that the Lord is always with us. He has promised never to leave or forsake us. He tells us we are His little lambs and He is our great Shepherd. He upholds us with His righteous right hand. He leads us along still waters and restores our soul. These are just a few of the promises of God regarding the care He provides for His children.

The next time you need some confidence, instead of worrying or trying to muster it up on your own, seek God. Read 2 Corinthians 12:9, and remember that in your weakness, God shows up to be your strength. He will be your confidence.

God, be my confidence when this world brings me situations
in which I feel insecure or inadequate. Thank You.

PEOPLE PLEASER VERSUS GOD PLEASER

We are not trying to please people but God, who tests our hearts.
1 Thessalonians 2:4 niv

Much of what we say and do stems from our desire to be accepted by others. We strive to make a certain impression, to shed the best light possible on ourselves. Wanting to be viewed as successful, we may decide to exaggerate, embellish, or even lie. It's difficult to be true to ourselves when we care so much about the acceptance and opinions of others. Impression management is hard work, so it's good to know God has a better plan!

Rather than being driven by the opinions of others, strive to live your life for God alone and to please Him above all else. God knows our hearts. He perceives things as they truly are. We cannot fool Him. When we allow ourselves to be real before Him, it doesn't matter what others think. If the God of the universe has accepted us, then who cares about someone else's opinion?

It is impossible to please both God and man. We must make a choice. Man looks at the outward appearance, but God looks at the heart. Align your heart with His. Let go of impression management that focuses on outward appearance. Receive God's unconditional love, and enjoy the freedom to be yourself before Him!

Dear Lord, may I live for You alone. Help me transition
from a people pleaser to a God pleaser. Amen.

GUILT-FREE

So now there is no condemnation
for those who belong to Christ Jesus.
ROMANS 8:1 NLT

Every one of us has messed up—some of us big-time. Fortunately, we serve the God of second chances.

He tells us in 1 John 1:9, "If we confess our sins, he is faithful and just and will forgive us our sins and purify us from all unrighteousness" (NIV).

When we confess our failures, repent, and move on, God wipes those mistakes away—He sees the children He created, who are washed in the blood of Jesus.

"Therefore," Romans 8:1 says, "[there is] now no condemnation (no adjudging guilty of wrong) for those who are in Christ Jesus, who live [and] walk not after the dictates of the flesh, but after the dictates of the Spirit" (AMPC).

Whatever we've done wrong, let's stop condemning ourselves. If we've confessed those sins, there is no need for our feelings of guilt.

Guilt has held back the blessings of God long enough! Let it go! Have faith in the blood that cleanses *all* sins—past, present, and future.

"Even if we feel guilty, God is greater than our feelings, and he knows everything" (1 John 3:20 NLT).

Father God, I thank You that You have forgiven me. Help me to forgive myself—
and to let go of the guilt that keeps me from becoming the person You say that I am.
Your Word is true, and I choose to believe what You say over what I feel.

BURDEN-BEARING

For I satisfy the weary ones and refresh everyone who languishes.
JEREMIAH 31:25 NASB

What kind of burdens are you carrying today? Finances, health, work, family cares, children—they're all burdens we take on, thinking we have to work out all the problems and find the solutions.

Jesus tells us, "If you are tired from carrying heavy burdens, come to me and I will give you rest. Take the yoke I give you. Put it on your shoulders and learn from me. I am gentle and humble, and you will find rest. This yoke is easy to bear, and this burden is light" (Matthew 11:28–30 CEV). While these verses primarily refer to the burden of guilt and shame over sin and our inability to release that burden on our own, a secondary meaning applies to the burdens we take on ourselves. . .by not trusting God's sovereignty in every area of our lives.

Several times in scripture, we humans are compared to sheep. Sheep are not burden-bearing animals. You don't see shepherds loading them up like mules, camels, and horses. Neither are we required to take on burdens. The fact is that many times in God's Word we're encouraged to roll every burden onto *Him*.

The promised result is God's rest—His peace, His refreshing of our spirits—in spite of any problem we face. When we submit to His yoke, we find that the burden truly is light and easy to bear. No longer languishing, we find ourselves refreshed, walking forward in His strength.

Father God, may we heed Jesus' invitation today, knowing that
Your desire is to do all things for our good and Your glory.

....

....

....

....

....

....

....

"PERFECT PEACE AND REST"

For thus said the Lord God, the Holy One of Israel, "In returning and rest you shall be saved; in quietness and in trust shall be your strength." But you were unwilling.
ISAIAH 30:15 ESV

Some of the saddest words in the Bible are found at the end of Isaiah 30:15: "But you were unwilling." Here the Lord sets before His people a simple formula to reverse the extreme difficulties of life they were experiencing. By returning to God's ways and resting in Him, they could be safe from the enemies who sought to destroy them. In quieting their spirits and trusting in God, they could be strengthened for the battles ahead. But they were unwilling. Instead they wanted to flee God's presence.

Frances Ridley Havergal's devotion to God throughout her short life is seen in her many hymns. The nineteenth-century English woman's life was riddled with pain and sickness, yet she sought the Lord through it all. In her hymn "Like a River Glorious," she depicts the peace and rest God offers as a mighty river, growing fuller and deeper each day. The refrain summarizes God's promise to each of us: "Stayed upon Jehovah, hearts are fully blest; finding, as He promised, perfect peace and rest."

Father, I'm tired of trying to outrun my problems. May Your peace flow through me like a mighty river, bringing rest to my soul.

MAKE A CHOICE

Do not let your hearts be troubled.
You believe in God; believe also in me.
JOHN 14:1 NIV

Some days are full of joy and peace; others are not. When we face the inevitable difficult days in life, we must choose how we respond. We bring light to the darkest of days when we turn our faces to God. Sometimes we must let in trusted friends and family members to help us on our journeys toward solving our problems.

David knew much distress and discomfort when he cried out, "God is our refuge and strength" (Psalm 46:1 NIV). Matthew Henry's commentary says of Psalm 46, "Through Christ, we shall be conquerors. . . . He is a Help, a present Help, a Help found, one whom we have found to be so; a Help at hand, one that is always near; we cannot desire a better, nor shall we ever find the like in any creature."

Knowing that Christ is at the center of our battles—and that we can trust Him—lends peace and stills the weakest of hearts. Rely on Him to lead you through the darkest days.

Oh Lord, still my troubled heart. Let me learn to rely on You in
all circumstances. Thank You, Father, for Your everlasting love.

FIRM FOOTING

*The Sovereign LORD is my strength; he makes my feet like
the feet of a deer, he enables me to tread on the heights.*
HABAKKUK 3:19 NIV

Violence and destruction surrounded the prophet Habakkuk as his disobedient nation, Judah, fell under the heel of the warlike Chaldeans. Though he called out to God, the faithful prophet seemed to get no answer.

Habakkuk recognized God's judgment in this attack by a pagan people, yet he still looked to his Lord for mercy. This verse of hopeful words declares that Habakkuk's strength still came from the same Lord who used His power to humble His people.

Are we feeling tired today? Drained spiritually and financially? Do the warriors of disease, depression, or despair attack us? Let's follow in Habakkuk's footsteps: when destruction stares us in the face, let's make God our strength.

Our Lord's power offers us a firm footing no matter what dangerous places we travel through. He will carry us safely over high mountain trails or through deep swamps.

Though He sometimes sets a difficult path before us, God does not leave us to walk alone. In His strength, wherever we go, we cannot fall.

*Lord, in my own power I'm extremely frail. I stumble daily.
Help me to cling to You, trusting that You'll safely lead
me through. Your strength alone gives me firm footing.*

A SURE FOUNDATION

*Now faith is confidence in what we hope
for and assurance about what we do not see.*
HEBREWS 11:1 NIV

This definition of faith is not "wishing upon a star." No, Hebrews 11 describes faith as a firm confidence in God's promise and provision. He can—and will—perform a work in us for our good and His glory, whatever trials or heartaches occur along the way.

People speak of "blind faith," but real, biblical faith has three important elements. First, true faith is grounded in the knowledge of God that we discover in scripture. As we study God's Word, the facts become clear, and we move to the second element: acceptance of the evidence, or belief. The third element of faith is trust, including repentance from our sins and reliance upon our God. As our understanding grows, we actually realize that, from start to finish, our faith and repentance are gifts from God.

Are you certain of God's design for your life amid any assignment? If not, try to view your duty from God's perspective, as an opportunity to become more like your Savior. Jesus fulfilled the role of servant every day, ultimately giving His life to bring us into His kingdom.

Today you can stand in faith, being sure of what you hope for and certain of what you do not see. It's the only way to live.

*Lord, You are full of mercy and grace. I thank You for this gift of faith.
Increase it, I pray, and make me more fruitful for You.*

I'M WEARY, LORD

The LORD is the strength of my life.
PSALM 27:1 KJV

All of us have moments in our journey when we feel drained—when we can't take another step. We have difficult days, trying times, and perplexing periods in life. But we can be thankful that our God stands ready and willing to give us comfort and strength—if we'll just open our hearts and let Him.

We're tempted to "burn the candle at both ends," sapping our energy to the breaking point. But then we're of no use to anyone. We're spent, poured out. Now is the time to learn to place first things first.

We might have to say no to something we simply cannot do or, as hard as it may be, delegate responsibilities to others. Then we rest our weary frames in the hands of the Almighty. He knows our limits, though there are times we wonder if He's overestimating our abilities. But our faithful Father sees the big picture and shoulders our yoke with us.

Focus on the Lord. Ask Him for wisdom to prioritize the duties you have. Ask Him for the strength to fulfill your responsibilities. Send up a silent plea for rest and rejuvenation, and then rejoice when He answers.

Dear Lord, let me find my strength in You.
Teach me to rest in Your love and leadership.

SECURE

For I hold you by your right hand—I, the LORD your God.
And I say to you, "Don't be afraid. I am here to help you."
ISAIAH 41:13 NLT

Like children, we can lift up our hands and grasp our Father's firm hand whenever fear threatens to overtake our lives. It doesn't matter whether we have a sin to conquer or an unsolvable crisis. God always stands there for us.

When our troubles lie beyond human solution, we are not cast adrift on a sea of woes. Nor when we face purely practical, ordinary troubles are we left to our own devices. Jesus walks at our sides, ready to intervene or comfort us. Though any problem may toss us around a bit, anxieties need not overwhelm us completely.

No fear permanently damages us when our Father stands beside us. Let's grab His hand, knowing He will protect and love us. He never fails.

Do we need more security than that?

No matter how protective my earthly father was, I know, Lord, that I can trust You to help me as I face so many overwhelming challenges. You are sovereign over the whole earth and every life on it, including mine. I trust that You will never fail me.

DON'T GIVE IN

But you'll welcome us with open arms when we run for cover to you.
Let the party last all night! Stand guard over our celebration. You are
famous, GOD, for welcoming God-seekers, for decking us out in delight.
PSALM 5:11–12 MSG

From time to time, we can lose hope and become discouraged despite all the blessings surrounding us. When this happens, we need to remember Paul's words about the certainty of God's promises and realize that our God will never forsake us.

When we have those down-in-the-dumps days, we should encircle ourselves with encouragers, Christian friends who can hold up our arms—like Moses (see Exodus 17:11–12)—when we're unable to continue the journey. We can reach for God's Word, which breathes life into our spirits. Moments of prayer will connect us to the Life-giver and refresh us.

Worry and discouragement are spiritual traps that sap our energy and cover us with a cloud of gloom. These evil twins can be dispelled by praise. Turn on the radio, hum an old hymn, read a psalm aloud. We can choose to praise and look for joy in spite of our circumstances. David did. Paul and Silas did. We can, too.

God has promised to give us peace and joy in spite of our trials and struggles. Let's reach out to Him and shed our veil of darkness for a mantle of praise.

Heavenly Father, I lift my eyes to the heavens and ask for Your peace. Thank You for Your love and care. Thank You for standing by my side. I praise Your name.

NOURISHMENT

So then, just as you received Christ Jesus as Lord, continue to live your lives in him, rooted and built up in him, strengthened in the faith as you were taught, and overflowing with thankfulness.
COLOSSIANS 2:6–7 NIV

Dana's neighbor peeked over the fence, trying to figure out the strange contraptions next door. Three-tiered towers of cone-shaped containers holding. . .what? A limp, spindly plant of some kind. Whatever they were, they didn't look like they were going to make it.

Turns out they were strawberry plants growing in a fluffy artificial soil. Dana fed them through tubes delivering fertilized water directly to the roots of each plant. In time, the plants grew healthy and productive, with roots deep and strong. The continual input of nutrients strengthened the once-scrawny plants. An overflow of plump red berries resulted.

We're a lot like those strawberry plants, strengthened and built up in the Lord when we dig deep into His Word. Like that fluffy artificial soil, our surroundings may seem unstable—but God's sustaining, living water is what makes all the difference.

His power, His influence, His dynamism girds us up to accomplish the tasks at hand each day. Our anemic efforts, our weary bodies, and our lackluster minds receive the needed vitality and vigor to meet each day's demands with power and enthusiasm. And an overflow of thanksgiving is the result.

Lord, please nourish my inner being with Your Word and Your presence. Gird me up for today's tasks, and help me to be thankful.

DAY WRITER

All the days ordained for me were written
in your book before one of them came to be.
PSALM 139:16 NIV

Why does Almighty God, a being with unlimited health at His disposal, write pain into today?

Why does God, initiator of various infinite excitements, write drudgery—the tedious, repetitive routine of caring for those who can't care for themselves—into this day for me?

These questions nettle us.

In John 9:1–3 Jesus' disciples saw a desperate blind man and asked the question that nettled them. "Rabbi, whose sin caused this suffering?"

"This happened so the glory of God might be displayed in his life," Jesus replied.

Jesus' answer shifted the conversation's focus from a perplexing human question to a satisfying divine answer. Then Jesus acted to display God's glory.

Like the disciples, we ask questions rooted in human perspective. God's answer helps us look at life from His perspective. Maybe God wrote our pain so His glory could be displayed in our lives today.

Allow God to shift your focus from your pain to His glory. He promises to show up and arrange circumstances so He is your hero. Pain may lead to a cascade of spiritual blessing. Drudgery may be the backdrop for extravagant compassion.

The God who writes the pain is with us. He writes with purpose and love—and with our supreme benefit in mind.

Dear God, Author of life and each day, help me trust You with my pain.
I beg You to take it away—but if my pain brings You glory, I ask You
to take my focus off myself and help me turn my thoughts to You.

BLESSING TO OTHERS

*From the day Joseph was put in charge of his master's household
and property, the LORD began to bless Potiphar's household for Joseph's sake.
All his household affairs ran smoothly, and his crops and livestock flourished.*
GENESIS 39:5 NLT

Joseph was a man who honored the Lord in all he did. Everything Joseph did was done "heartily, as to the Lord, and not unto men" (Colossians 3:23 KJV).

The household of Potiphar, an Egyptian official, was blessed because of Joseph. His own brothers, who had sold him into slavery, were blessed. The entire nation of Egypt—the world power of the day—was blessed.

Joseph lived centuries before Paul wrote his letter to the Colossians, but he clearly knew in his heart that he was to serve with all his might. That brought glory to God—and, as a result, Joseph became the second-in-command of all Egypt. He literally rose from prison to palace.

There's a lesson here for us. Whatever we do should be done "heartily, as to the Lord, and not unto men." Just as God blessed Joseph and those around him, God will be faithful to bless us and those we care for.

*Father, I thank You for the blessings You bestow not only on me
but also on my loved ones as I faithfully seek You. Help me to be the
very best I can be. Let Your faithfulness shine through me.*

HE ENJOYS YOU

The LORD your God is in your midst, a mighty one who will save;
he will rejoice over you with gladness; he will quiet you
by his love; he will exult over you with loud singing.
ZEPHANIAH 3:17 ESV

Memory is a powerful part of each one of us. Perhaps you can see your father cheering you on in a sports event, or you remember your mother stroking your feverish forehead while you lay sick in bed. With those mental pictures comes a recollection of emotion—how good it felt to be cheered and encouraged—how comforting it was to be loved and attended.

Zephaniah's words remind us that God is our loving parent. Our mighty Savior offers us a personal relationship, loving and rejoicing over us, His children, glad that we live and move in Him. He is the Lord of the universe, and yet He will quiet our restless hearts and minds with His tender love. He delights in our lives and celebrates our union with Him. We can rest in His affirmation and love no matter what circumstances surround us.

Lord, help me remember that You are always with me and that You delight in me.
Remind me that I am Your child and that You enjoy our relationship.

ACTIVELY WAIT ON HIM

Wait on the Lord: be of good courage, and he shall strengthen thine heart: wait, I say, on the Lord.
PSALM 27:14 KJV

Do you feel overwhelmed with the demands of your life?

Are you frustrated by your circumstances or weary in your service?

Then think of David.

Having already been anointed king by Samuel, David was running for his life. David's foes, followers of the murderous, disobedient King Saul, were out for his life.

But David didn't fear. He knew that God would hide him, protect him, and eventually set his feet on a rock. In the midst of the trouble, David praised God.

David ended this confident psalm by saying we should "wait on the Lord."

Notice he says "wait *on*," not "wait *for*." Sometimes we miss the difference. "Waiting on" someone is active, like waiting on tables. "Waiting for" someone is passive, like waiting for a package to be delivered.

As we "wait on" the Lord, we need to actively seek Him, behold Him, and praise Him. As we do this, we'll gain confidence and strength in Him.

Father, my life is so busy that I sometimes think I need to stop so You can catch up. But I know I never have to "wait for" You. You're always with me. Let me wait on You. In this I will find the strength to go on.

A NEW DAY

The faithful love of the LORD never ends! His mercies never cease.
Great is his faithfulness; his mercies begin afresh each morning.
LAMENTATIONS 3:22–23 NLT

Did you have a rough day yesterday?

Sometimes it feels like we have more than our share of things that go wrong. Often we just don't handle those problems the way we wish we would. Then more doubts and concerns loom on our horizon.

But this is a new day, full of grace and promise. One day is separated from another by night, and with the morning light comes a renewal of God's grace and strength to carry on. We might use all our human resources—all our grace, our strength, our patience, our ability—in a single day. But don't worry. The Lord is faithful, and He'll give us a whole new supply of every good thing for the new day.

Before this day even began, God knew what we would face, what we would need to get through—and He provided for that. Drawing on *His* assets—His grace, His faithfulness, His gifts for us—we'll have plenty of strength.

As we trust and praise God, we are able to draw on all His blessings for today—and all the days to come.

Thank You, Lord, that Your mercies are new every morning. I thank You for providing me with all I will need for this day. Please remind me to rely on You.

HOLY-SPIRIT PRAYERS

*We do not know how to pray as we should, but the Spirit Himself intercedes
for us with groanings too deep for words; and He who searches
the hearts knows what the mind of the Spirit is, because He
intercedes for the saints according to the will of God.*

ROMANS 8:26–27 NASB

Many times the burdens and troubles of our lives are too complicated to understand. It's difficult for us to put them into words, let alone know how to pray
for what we need. And unless we know someone who has been through similar
circumstances, we can feel isolated and alone.

But we can always take comfort in knowing that the Holy Spirit knows, understands, and pleads our case before the throne of God the Father. Our groans become
words in the Holy Spirit's mouth, turning our mute prayers into praise and interces-
sion "according to the will of God."

We can be encouraged, knowing that our deepest longings and desires, maybe
unknown even to us, are presented before the God who knows us and loves us completely. Our names are engraved on His heart and hands. He never forgets us; He
intervenes in all things for our good and His glory.

*Father, I thank You for the encouragement these verses bring.
May I always be aware of the Holy Spirit's interceding on my behalf.*

ABOVE THE CLOUDS

The engulfing waters threatened me, the deep surrounded me....
But you, LORD my God, brought my life up from the pit.
When my life was ebbing away, I remembered you.
JONAH 2:5–7 NIV

As a plane ascended, passengers peered out the windows at the swirling gray mist shrouding their jet. Nothing was visible; all was barren and bleak. In a few minutes, though, the plane broke through the clouds, startling passengers' eyes with shafts of light. Above the clouds the sun shone brightly.

Sometimes we have our heads in the clouds. All we see is the swirling gray mist, the gloom and sadness. We become myopic and focus on our circumstances, forgetting that above it all, our God sits upon the throne, shining light and piercing the darkness.

Remember Jonah inside the belly of the great fish? He saw no light. He saw no way out of his circumstances. Yet Almighty God delivered him and used him for His glory. There was light despite the darkness, hope instead of despair.

When life knocks us for a loop, we must focus on God's promises. We must rely on His words. Evil exists and hard times can envelop us, but our heavenly Father still reigns. He is the Light.

Oh Lord, bless Your name.
Thank You for Your watch-care even when I don't see it.

ANSWERING GOD'S CALL TO CARE

And she went and did according to the saying of Elijah:
and she, and he, and her house, did eat many days.
1 KINGS 17:15 KJV

Before God sent Elijah from the brook Cherith, He had already commanded a widow in Zarephath to sustain the prophet.

We don't know if God did that by a specific revelation or by some inner prompting. But we can tell from the account in 1 Kings that the woman recognized Elijah as a Jew who followed Jehovah.

As Elijah arrived at the gate of Zarephath, the widow seemed unaware of God's full plan. She was preparing to make her last meal, but the stranger offered her a choice: she could feed herself and her son first, or she could feed *him* first, believing that he was speaking the truth when he said her oil and meal would last until the drought ended.

The woman chose to serve Elijah first—and God blessed her. He kept her alive through the famine and eventually gave her back her son's life.

Like that widow, we often have a choice in caring for the people God sends into our lives. They may be members of our family or our church—or they might be total strangers, the people most easily overlooked.

Like the widow of Zarephath, we receive unexpected benefits when we choose to serve. Answer God's call to care for others—even strangers—and be blessed.

Father, give me ears to hear Your command to serve. Let me be discerning
so I can be a minister to all those You want me to help.

AN EXTRAVAGANT GOD

Change your life, not just your clothes. Come back to God, your God.
And here's why: God is kind and merciful. He takes a deep breath,
puts up with a lot, this most patient God, extravagant in love.
JOEL 2:13 MSG

There are times when we are exhausted and discouraged when we allow our minds to roam to dark places. Despair and disappointment set in. A woe-is-me attitude prevails. How do we rise from the doldrums? How do we continue? We turn our faces toward the Lord God and know that He is in control.

Scripture tells of God's mercy and loving-kindness. It speaks to us to come back to God. This doesn't necessarily mean a change of circumstances but a change of heart. And this change is a choice we intentionally make. It's not necessary to be in a church building or revival tent. While many changes happen there, ours can be in our closets, our cars, our offices. We reach inwardly to the Highest and ask for His mercy. And scripture says He is merciful.

Focusing on the negative—choosing despair—doesn't bring life. Voluntarily focusing on Jesus will. Praise Him for all your blessings: they are there—look for them! Some might be tiny, others magnificent. But they're all because of our Lord Jesus Christ. He is a most patient God and extravagant in His love.

Heavenly Father, I praise Your name. You are extravagant in Your love,
filling me to overflowing! I am grateful for all You've done.

BE A GOD PLEASER

Am I now trying to win the approval of human beings, or of God?
Or am I trying to please people? If I were still trying to please people,
I would not be a servant of Christ.
GALATIANS 1:10 NIV

Sometimes we work ourselves to the bone because we have no choice. Other times, we do it to win the approval of others.

Today, let's be honest with ourselves. Are we run-down? Worn out? If that's the result of situations we can't control, let's ask the Lord to give us the strength we need to keep going. But if we're exhausted because we're afraid of letting people down or hurting their her feelings, it might be time to reassess. If we're up to our eyebrows in work, overlooking other options for the people under our care, then we might be caught up in the "people-pleaser" game.

Here's how the game works: We do our best to make others happy—at any expense. Our health, our finances, our time. We sacrifice in unbalanced ways because we're concerned about what people will think of us.

Today, let's aim to be God pleasers. Let's do the things *He* calls us to—nothing more and nothing less.

Lord, You see my heart. You know what struggles I have in accomplishing
these tasks. Redirect my thoughts, Father, to pleasing You rather than others.

THE BEST-LAID PLANS

In their hearts humans plan their course,
*but the L*ORD *establishes their steps.*
PROVERBS 16:9 NIV

Why is it so hard to do the things we intend to do? We create to-do lists and plan our agendas, but the next thing we know, life interrupts. The reality is that we don't *have* any control—God does.

When all our intentions for the day are turned upside down, what can we do? Why not pause and turn your heart to God in prayer? We can set aside our own agendas and trust Him to show us the way. We can recognize that He is in charge of our next steps.

Sure, we should still make plans to accomplish the things that need to be done. But we need to leave enough flexibility in those plans for God's ultimate direction. He's the only One who really knows what lies ahead. And He will lead us in our daily steps.

God of our steps, You know my plans, hopes, and dreams for each day. I rely only
on You to shine Your light on each of my steps on the path laid out before me.

LOOK AROUND

Come and see the works of God; He is awesome
in His doing toward the sons of men.
PSALM 66:5 NKJV

We tend to think of encouragement as coming in the way of cards, phone calls, gifts, or efforts performed on our behalf. Isn't it wonderful how God uses people to encourage us? But when the cards or calls don't come, we're wise to look at the other ways God can send us encouragement.

First, He uplifts us through His Word. Just by reading the Bible, we're reminded of the grace and love God has for us. Then there's His creation. Watching a bird fly, seeing a squirrel scramble up a tree, and observing a beautiful flower or a wonderful sunrise are just a few ways God reminds us of His power. Encouragement can also be found by remembering what God has done for us.

If it's been awhile since you received a phone call, visit, or card, don't grow discouraged, thinking that God isn't aware of your needs. He's creative in His encouragement—just take the time to look for it.

Dear God, I thank You for all the ways You encourage me. May I not overlook
Your blessings because they didn't come in the form I expected.

CHOSEN

Before I formed you in the womb I knew you, before you were born
I set you apart; I appointed you as a prophet to the nations.
JEREMIAH 1:5 NIV

What an awesome thought! God said that before He formed Jeremiah in his mother's womb, He knew him. He *chose* Jeremiah. God separated him from everyone else to perform a specific task, and He consecrated him for that purpose. Wow!

We can be sure that if God did that for Jeremiah, He did it for each one of us. In fact, the apostle Paul said, "He chose us in Him before the foundation of the world, that we would be holy and blameless before Him. In love He predestined us to adoption as sons through Jesus Christ to Himself, according to the kind intention of His will, to the praise of the glory of His grace, which He freely bestowed on us in the Beloved" (Ephesians 1:4–6 NASB).

Nothing about us or our circumstances surprises God. He knew about everything before we were born. And He ordained that we should walk in those ways because we are uniquely qualified by Him to do so. He approved us because He chose us for our specific situation. And He equipped us for every trial and difficulty we will ever face in life. What an awesome God we serve!

Father, the thought that You chose me before the foundation of the world
and set me apart for a specific calling is humbling. You are so good.
May I go forward with a renewed purpose in life.

DO GOOD AND DO WELL

Trust in the Lord, and do good; so shalt thou dwell in the land,
and verily thou shalt be fed.
PSALM 37:3 KJV

It's a fact of life: once you start meeting the needs of the people around you, you'll always find more people around you with needs.

This is no surprise, of course. Jesus Himself said, "The poor you will always have with you" (Mark 14:7 NIV). There will always be people who need financial, physical, or spiritual help.

As much as we may want to help everyone with a need, we can't. We can't provide food to every hungry person in our town. We can't keep every disabled children from the world's cruelty. We can't care for every widow and orphan we meet.

And we aren't called to do so. Paul wrote, "As we have therefore opportunity, let us do good unto all men, especially unto them who are of the household of faith" (Galatians 6:10 KJV).

We must have faith that the Lord will bring those who need us most into our lives. And we must trust Him to provide for us. As we do good to those around us, He will meet our needs. "He that giveth unto the poor shall not lack" (Proverbs 28:27 KJV).

Open your eyes to the needs around you, and trust in the Lord. As you care for others, He will care for you.

Father, sometimes I don't think I can take care of one more person!
My resources are already stretched. Please give me the faith to stretch out
my hands to the needy, knowing that You will provide my needs as I minister.

KICK BACK AND REFRESH

Ask and you will receive, and your joy will be complete.
JOHN 16:24 NIV

Is your life the American norm: hustle and bustle and stress-laden? Do you find yourself "coming and going"? In a rat race? Then you need to find a way to kick back and relax. It might only be a three-minute break in your busy schedule, but you have to stay healthy. One of the best ways to relax is through laughter.

Studies show that belly laughs result in muscle relaxation. While you laugh, the muscles that do not participate in the belly laugh relax. After you finish laughing, those muscles involved in the laughter start to relax. So the action takes place in two stages. Laughter also aids in diminishing pain, if by nothing more than providing a distraction. Laughter is free and has no negative side effects. The dictionary defines *laugh* this way: "to find amusement or pleasure in something; to be of a kind that inspires joy."

Joy! The word *joy* or *joyful* is used over two hundred times in the Bible. Find those passages and meditate on one each day. Seek out a source of joy. Look for things that are joy-producing: a funny sitcom with Lucy and Ethel or Moe and Curly. A joke in a magazine. A child's laughter can be contagious. Ask God for laughter to relax.

Dear Lord, so much in my life is hectic. Give me the opportunity to take a breath, slow down, and rejoice. Thank You.

CELEBRATE GOD'S GREATNESS

"Our Lord, we are thankful. . . . Because of your wonderful deeds we
will sing your praises everywhere on earth." Sing, people of Zion!
Celebrate the greatness of the holy Lord of Israel. God is here to help you.
ISAIAH 12:4–6 CEV

Intimately acquainted with physical difficulties since birth, a woman named Ruth learned early in life to rely on God for strength. She was normally a quiet, reserved woman, but when the opportunity arose to praise her Savior, she boldly proclaimed His mighty acts in her life. Her life was a celebration of praise to the glory and greatness of her God.

In today's scripture passage, the people of Israel were facing the most powerful army in the known world. Sennacherib boldly proclaimed what he would do to those who foolishly put their trust in God. But the inhabitants of Jerusalem chose to follow their king and trust wholly in their God to deliver them. And He did! Soon this prophecy proclaimed by Isaiah became fact.

How about you? Are you thankful for life? For your circumstances? For the blessings God bestows on you daily? For the difficulties? Today, let's celebrate God's greatness, because He "is here to help you."

Father God, I thank You for saving me, for delivering me from sin's penalty and power and—one day soon—from sin's presence. Thank You for Your grace to live each day, to serve You in my humanness. May I sing of Your wonderful deeds to all the world.

THE BLESSINGS OF WAITING

Blessed are those who listen to me,
watching daily at my doors, waiting at my doorway.
PROVERBS 8:34 NIV

We wait for other people. We wait in line at the grocery store. We wait to see what the next medical test will show. We wait quietly for our loved ones.

Waiting is part of life—but it isn't easy. When nothing seems to be happening, we can become impatient and anxious. We want things to start moving!

But waiting can be a form of activity. Waiting creates a pause that, if used correctly, can help us to linger and to listen. We can stop and collect our thoughts. We can take a few deep breaths and rest in God's care, even if we can't find the words or the energy to talk with Him.

Waiting allows us time to absorb our surroundings and enjoy a quiet moment. We can savor the sights, listen intently to the sounds, and touch base with our emotions. We can drink in all that is occurring around us instead of gulping it down.

Downtime allows us to open our hearts to be with God. Each wait-and-see moment holds His promises and blessings, because God waits and watches with us.

Lord, waiting is so difficult. Be with me as I wait,
and open my eyes to see the blessings in these pauses of life.

....

....

....

....

....

....

....

....

....

OUT OF THE PIT

God rescued us from dead-end alleys and dark dungeons. He's set us up in the
kingdom of the Son he loves so much, the Son who got us out of the pit
we were in, got rid of the sins we were doomed to keep repeating.
COLOSSIANS 1:13–14 MSG

It was as if he'd fallen into a deep, dark hole. Sleep, withdrawal, and numbness were his coping mechanisms. Going through the motions, trapped in despair, stuck in the ugliness of his sin—he seemed helpless to make the necessary changes within himself. He'd dealt with these same battles years before, thinking he'd conquered them. Yet here they were again, creeping through the chambers of his heart and mind and wreaking havoc on his spirit.

The message of the Gospel doesn't leave any of us there, trapped in sin and misery with no hope of rescue. God sent His Rescuer, Jesus Christ, who plucks us out of the dungeon of despair, transferring us into His kingdom of light. It's a message of hope that says we are not consigned to our habitual ruts.

Have the struggles of life led you into bad, even sinful, habits? Those dead-end alleys, so void of purpose, aren't the place to be. We walk in God's bright and beautiful kingdom. Get out of that pit, striding confidently toward Him, enjoying life to its fullest.

Glory to You, Jesus! You have rescued me from the pit and lifted me
to Your kingdom of real life and victory. Help me to walk in that truth today.

TO REST, KEEP GOING

And he said, My presence shall go
with thee, and I will give thee rest.
EXODUS 33:14 KJV

If you think your lot in life is difficult, imagine being Moses, stuck in the desert with a million people that you must lead to the promised land.

And if that's not tough enough, God has just told you that although you are supposed to get all those rebellious people marching again, He is not going to go in their midst because He's ready to consume them for their resistance.

Moses knew he couldn't proceed. He couldn't take care of all those people without God's guidance and provision.

So Moses did what any wise person would do: he communed with God. He humbly appealed to God's character and reputation.

The Father relented and promised Moses His presence and His rest.

And Moses went.

While our jobs are not as great as the one Moses had, we can learn from his example. When faced with a difficult situation, instead of complaining, we must *commune.*

And then we must go. God goes with us as we are going.

As we go with His guidance, He will give us rest. His rest is more than just a chance to put our feet up. It's a quiet confidence and inner peace, knowing that we are doing what God wants us to do.

Find rest today—commune, then continue, keeping a peaceful pace with Him.

Dear Father, You work in amazing ways—with You the strength comes in weakness;
the rest, in activity. Refresh me today as I care for those around me.

DO NOT BE AFRAID

Do not be afraid, for I have ransomed you. I have called you by name; you are mine.
When you go through deep waters, I will be with you. When you go through rivers
of difficulty, you will not drown. When you walk through the fire of oppression,
you will not be burned up; the flames will not consume you.
ISAIAH 43:1–2 NLT

Trials are inevitable, a part of life. God uses them to refine us, to burn up the dross, to mold us into the image of Jesus Christ. Even He was not immune to the difficulties of life. Jesus faced persecution, mocking, and death on the cross.

But in the midst of all trouble, Jesus walks beside us. He holds our heads above the water; He wraps us in flame-retardant clothing. We will not drown nor will we be consumed in the fiery furnace. Why? Because He ransomed us. He paid sin's penalty, He delivered us from the slave market of sin, and He calls us by name.

So when you feel like you're drowning in a flood of trouble and difficulty, breathe deeply and relax. Bodysurf across those waves. Even if the fire of oppression singes you, remember that His promise says you will not be consumed. He will satisfy your desires in the "scorched places" (Isaiah 58:11 NASB).

Face life with no fear—you are God's.

Father, may I keep my focus on You today—not on the water that threatens
to drown me or the fire that threatens to engulf me. I am Yours,
and You will enable me to walk through the dangers that surround me.

WITHOUT LOVE, I AM NOTHING

If I had such faith that I could move mountains,
but didn't love others, I would be nothing.
1 CORINTHIANS 13:2 NLT

If I can communicate effortlessly with doctors and nurses, comprehending difficult medical terminology, but have not love, I am only an annoying know-it-all.

If I claim to understand exactly how other people feel and can anticipate their needs without them having to say anything—even if I consider myself to be a mature Christian—when I do it without love, my service is meaningless.

If I give of myself daily, sacrificing my own needs and doing everything I can to help others, but have not love, my sacrifice is empty.

Love is patient when the person I love is impossibly slow. *Love is kind* when the one I love snaps at me. *It does not envy* those who seem better off than me. *It does not boast, it is not proud* of all the things I do for others. *It is not rude* even when I'm at the end of my rope. *It is not self-seeking* in spite of the fact that I give so much of myself. *It is not easily angered* when I'm sleep-deprived or feel taken advantage of. *It keeps no record of wrongs* no matter how unfair my situation seems. *Love does not delight in evil but rejoices with the truth* even when I am unable to see my circumstances clearly. *It always protects, always trusts, always hopes, always perseveres* even when I feel helpless, hopeless, and afraid.

Love never fails.

Dear God and Author of love, please teach me to love as You do.

DEMONSTRATE RIGHTEOUSNESS

I, the Lord, have called you to demonstrate my righteousness.
I will take you by the hand and guard you.
ISAIAH 42:6 NLT

It is often difficult to live a life that demonstrates Christ's righteousness before those we are closest to—our family members. Yet they may be the ones most needful of the Savior.

Living a consistent, righteous life before our spouses, our children, and our parents and siblings is challenging. We look at our homes as places we can relax, be "ourselves," and regroup for another day of stress. Yet it is in this environment that we are most tested. As we get older, our parents need help and support. Many of us may also have children still at home who require much of our attention. The stress of the "sandwich generation"—those caring for both oldsters and youngsters—is great.

But God is faithful. He doesn't require us to demonstrate Christ's love and righteous living without His help. Jesus told His disciples that when He left earth for heaven after His resurrection, God would send the Holy Spirit, our "Comforter" (John 14:26 KJV), to enable each of us to live righteous, godly lives. The apostle Peter declares that, when we accept salvation through Jesus Christ, we are equipped with all we need to live a godly life (2 Peter 1:3–4). Because of this we are able to demonstrate righteousness in the most stressful circumstances.

Father, You are so good! You allow trial and difficulty, stress and pain to enter our lives, but not without equipping us with the strength and abilities to live righteously before our families. Thank You, Lord.

OVERWHELMED BY LIFE

The waves of death swirled about me; the torrents of destruction
overwhelmed me.... In my distress I called to the LORD....
From his temple he heard my voice; my cry came to his ears.
2 SAMUEL 22:5, 7 NIV

Some days the "dailyness" of life seems like a never-ending grind. We get up, eat, work, rest—and do it again the next day. Then when tragedy strikes, we're swept up in grief. What once seemed doable now seems a huge challenge. Depression sinks its claws deep into our spirit. Fatigue sets in, and we are overwhelmed: life is hard. We may be tempted to question, "Is this all there is?"

Here's the good news: there's more. God never meant for us to simply exist. He created us for a specific purpose. He longs for us to make a difference and show others His love and grace. What's more, He never asked us to do life alone. When the waves of death swirl around us and the pounding rain of destruction threatens to overwhelm us, we can cry out to our heavenly Father, knowing that He will not let us drown. He will hear our voice, and He will send help.

So next time you feel that you can't put one foot in front of the other, ask God to send you His strength and energy. He will help you to live out your purpose in this chaotic world.

Lord, thank You for strengthening me when the "dailyness"
of life and its various trials threaten to overwhelm me.

UNEXPECTED REWARDS OF MERCY

*Then she fell on her face…and said unto him, Why have I found grace
in thine eyes…seeing I am a stranger? And Boaz answered…
It hath fully been shewed me, all that thou hast done unto
thy mother in law since the death of thine husband.*
RUTH 2:10–11 KJV

When Ruth the Moabite married into a family of Israelites, she had no idea what trials and blessings were ahead.

Her marriage was brief. Her husband died, as did her father- and brother-in-law. And then her grieving, bitter mother-in-law, Naomi, decided to return to Israel.

Would Ruth go home, or would she live among strangers with Naomi? Although she had seen sorrow in Elimelech's household, she had also seen faith. She knew Naomi's God was the true God, and she chose Him.

So she remained with Naomi, serving her as a faithful daughter.

Her mercy did not go unnoticed. The people of Bethlehem talked. By the time she arrived in Boaz's field, he already knew of all she had done for Naomi, so he offered her food and protection. He also blessed her, saying, "A full reward be given thee of the LORD" (Ruth 2:12 KJV).

Ruth had a fuller reward than she could have imagined. She married Boaz and became part of the lineage of Christ.

Our acts of mercy are never ignored by our Lord. In His time, He will give a full reward. As we sow, so shall we reap.

*Father, sometimes I sense no honor or reward as I serve. But I know
there is a greater reward coming. Let me remain faithful.*

CALMED BY HIS LOVE

The LORD your God is in your midst, a mighty one who will save;
he will rejoice over you with gladness; he will quiet you by his love;
he will exult over you with loud singing.

ZEPHANIAH 3:17 ESV

What is causing you unrest today? Inadequacy? Lack of strength? Poor finances?

God wants you to know that He is with you. He sees your circumstances, your concerns, your worries. And He wants you to know that He's the mighty one who will save you. He is rejoicing over you with gladness, exulting over you with loud singing. Why?

Because He loves you. And He wants to wrap you in His love that's like a thick comforter on a cold winter evening. He wants us to rest in His love. For only His love can calm the fear that hinders you from doing what He's tasked you to do.

God's love sent His Son to die for you that you might receive everything you need pertaining to life and godliness. His love enables you to keep on going even when you're ready to give up. His love allows you to rest, to gain strength, to be still in the midst of the storm that is raging all around you. The waters will not rise enough to drown you nor will the raging fire consume you.

Father, I thank You for the gift of Your love. It calms me, it soothes me, it gives me peace in the middle of the storm. Please fill me with Your love and peace today.

LASTING STRENGTH

Finally, be strong in the Lord and in his mighty power.
EPHESIANS 6:10 NIV

From where do we draw our strength? Do we think it comes from a good workout? Do we believe we'll be strong if we get enough sleep at night? Or eat a hearty breakfast? Those are all healthful energy boosters, but they do not provide the *real* strength that daily life requires.

Sometimes we need physical strength. Other times it's the strength that allows us to hold up under stress or sorrow. Or perhaps we need strength to battle feelings of frustration and impatience we find ourselves experiencing.

Whatever the reason for our need, the source of strength is always the same: God. His strength isn't temporary; it won't wear out over time. There's no waiting for Him to order in a fresh supply or worrying that He won't have enough. His strength is there continually, an outgrowth of His mighty power.

Stop reaching for the energy that fades—ask instead for the strength our God supplies.

Heavenly Father, from Your power You provide me with the strength I need each day. Help me to remember to call upon You.

JOY IN THE MORNING

All who seek the LORD will praise him.
Their hearts will rejoice with everlasting joy.
PSALM 22:26 NLT

How grand God is! He knows how dependent we are on Him for the everyday joy we need to carry on. And every day, He provides us with beauty all around to cheer and help us.

It may come through the beauty of flowers or the bright blue sky—or maybe the white snow covering the trees of a glorious winter wonderland. It may be through the smile of a child or the grateful face of the one we care for. Each and every day, the Lord has a special gift to remind us of whose we are and to generate the joy we need to succeed.

In our own pain and frustration, there are times when our eyes don't see the beauty God sends. But if we'll ask, He'll show us. God is faithful to build us up with everything we need to serve Him with joy. What an awesome God we serve!

Lord God, I thank You for Your joy; I thank You for
providing it every day to sustain me. I will be joyful in You.

A CHEERFUL HEART

Happy is he. . .whose hope is in the Lord his God.
PSALM 146:5 KJV

When we walk the road of life, cheerfulness is often a foreign feeling. Our responsibilities lay heavily on our hearts, miring us in the mundane. That's when we need an attitude check. We have to consciously make a choice to be cheerful. That doesn't mean our circumstances are any less difficult or trying. But we can choose, every day, to rise above them and smile.

In Proverbs 15:15 Solomon wrote, "The cheerful heart has a continual feast" (NIV). Solomon had probably gleaned this bit of wisdom from his father, King David. Who better than David, living in fear of constant pursuit, would know the importance of choosing happiness? In the midst of his darkest hours, he called on his God of hope. His obedience connected him with the Life-giver, the Lifeline, his Lord.

In His Word, God promises lives of abundance and joy—but we need to claim these promises. When we do, Jesus fills our spirits with His power and His love, which enable us to journey forth with hope. We receive this gift by giving Him the gift of our lives and hearts—a conscious choice. A choice that will change our lives.

This day, let's choose joy. Let's choose to be cheerful.

Dear Lord, today help me choose an attitude of cheerfulness.
Fill me with Your joy, hope, and peace. Help me to celebrate today.

CALMING THE STORM

The disciples went and woke him, saying, "Master, Master,
we're going to drown!" He got up and rebuked the wind and
the raging waters; the storm subsided, and all was calm.
LUKE 8:24 NIV

Ever feel like you're in over your head? Like you might go under at any point? Are the waves crashing? The winds howling? The thunder rumbling? Take heart—Jesus is in the business of calming storms. Even the most frightening ones.

It's not unusual to feel overwhelmed, especially when the boat of your life is rocking out of control. But Jesus stands at the helm, speaking with great authority to the wind and the waves. "Peace, be still!" He commands.

And as the realization sets in, peace like a river washes over you. He is with you! When you pass through the waters, you will not drown. The storm you're experiencing will subside. . .in time. Even while the thunders roar, know that His holy calm is coming.

He's more than able to calm whatever storm you're facing.

Dear Lord, I feel like the boat of my life has pitched back and forth.
So many times I've felt like I might drown! Father, I ask You to calm
this raging storm. Bring peace, Lord, as I rest in Your arms.

A QUIET PLACE

At daybreak, Jesus went out to a solitary place.
LUKE 4:42 NIV

Don't you find it interesting that Jesus, the Savior of the world, took time to slip away to a quiet place? He knew that this quiet, intimate time with His Father was absolutely essential.

With all the hustle and bustle of caring for someone in need, it's tough to sneak away for quiet time. But it's worth it! In those peaceful moments, we gain the strength we need for the tasks ahead. There in the arms of our loving Savior we find comfort, peace, and rest. We garner the courage and the tenacity to keep on keeping on, even when things are tough.

So when can *you* manage a few minutes of respite from the world? And where will it be? In the quiet of the morning in your bedroom? Soaking in a warm bubble bath? On a leisurely walk through a nearby park? In the car as you scurry from one place to another? Whenever and wherever, be sure to get away as often as you can. God will meet you in that place.

Dear Lord, remind me that when I draw near to You,
You draw near to me. Woo me daily into that quiet, solitary place—
away from the chaos and confusion. Let me rest my head on
Your shoulder and feel Your strong arms around me.

GOD'S PROVING GROUND

God said to Moses, "I'm going to rain bread down from the skies for you.
The people will go out and gather each day's ration. I'm going to
test them to see if they'll live according to my Teaching or not."
EXODUS 16:4 MSG

It seemed like such a simple test. The directions were clear; the time frame was easy enough to handle. No studying for the exam was needed. All the preparatory work was done.

Yet many failed.

With God fighting the battle, the people of Israel had escaped the tyranny of Egypt. Now they were a free people—but faced with nothing to eat, they wouldn't live to enjoy it. Or so they thought.

God told Moses that *He* would provide bread, manna from heaven. All the people had to do was gather it up each morning. A specific amount—no more, no less. And therein lay the test: Would the people follow the specific instructions each day? Or would they allow greed, laziness, or unbelief to rule their response?

God has promised to provide *our* every need—strength, wisdom, ability, daily bread. But many of us fail when it comes to appropriating the gift. We allow greed (desiring more than we need), laziness (trying to cut out the necessary exercise of prayer and the food of God's Word), or unbelief ("I need to help God out or it won't be enough") to keep us from His promises.

Today, let's purpose to succeed on God's proving ground.

Father, please help me to follow Your instructions carefully
so that I may experience the best You have for me today.

IT'S ALL GOOD

For the Lord God is a sun and shield: the Lord will give grace and glory:
no good thing will he withhold from them that walk uprightly.
PSALM 84:11 KJV

Our God is so much more than we can imagine. To help us understand Him, He gives us simple word pictures of Himself.

In this passage, God is a sun. Like the sun, He makes things grow so that we are sustained. But also like the sun, His rays can burn, purging our lives of evil.

God is also a shield. Although His glance could turn us to ash, He is able to protect us from Himself as well as from other things that could harm us.

As part of His protection, He gives us grace. He gives us favor and kindness. We are precious to Him; so precious that He makes us partakers of His glory (2 Corinthians 3:18).

This is our God! And He is good.

His goodness leads Him to give good things to His children. As we walk in obedience, we can trust that the difficulties of our lives are good because they come from the hand of a good God who sustains and protects us.

If a situation in your life doesn't seem good, don't doubt. That crisis or trial really is good because God promises to cause all things to work together for good.

Because God is in control, it's all good.

Father, sometimes the trials of my life don't look very good to me. But I must trust You, because You are good. Thank You for always working for my good.

EXERCISE! FIVE REASONS WHY

Don't you know that you yourselves are
God's temple and that God's Spirit dwells in your midst?
1 CORINTHIANS 3:16 NIV

You're busy. So trying to squeeze exercise into your day seems to be an impossible task. But physical activity is an investment that pays immeasurable dividends. Here are five reasons why daily exercise is a wise idea:

1. It's a great stress reliever. Exercise helps fight depression, in part because it releases chemicals in our brains that make us feel good.

2. It's good for your body. Obesity, heart trouble, diabetes, high blood pressure. . .you may be caring for someone who is suffering the effects of one of these diseases. Being ill is no fun—plus it's expensive and time-consuming, and it robs joy from your life. Squeeze in just three ten-minute sessions of exercise every day to help ward off disease.

3. It's easy. Getting enough exercise can be as simple as parking farther away from the grocery store, taking the stairs instead of the elevator, or doing some crunches in front of the television. With a little creativity and resourcefulness, your exercise options are virtually unlimited.

4. It improves your energy level and your quality of sleep. People who exercise have more energy when they're not exercising and sleep better when their heads finally hit the pillow. Who wouldn't benefit from that?

5. It honors God. God's Word calls our bodies "temples." He has entrusted these temples into our care, and when we care for our bodies, we are being good stewards. We demonstrate our thanks for this magnificent creation.

Father, I thank You for my body that enables me to do so much.
Help me to make caring for it a top priority.

....

....

....

....

....

GIVING THANKS

*It is good to proclaim your unfailing love in
the morning, your faithfulness in the evening.*
PSALM 92:2 NLT

Do you feel like giving thanks today? Do you recognize your many blessings? Your eyes may have opened this morning to situations and circumstances that don't inspire joy, but in spite of the worry and uncertainty, this day is a treasure. You're alive; you drew a breath when you awoke. Praise God!

Each day is a special gift to be savored and celebrated. God has created this time for us—and He's given us too many blessings to count. An attitude of praise and celebration will lift our spirits and help us commune with Him.

So look for the good things this day—the treasures. Sing a song in the shower or hum a tune over the washing machine. Whisper a prayer of gratitude before you turn out the light. Recognize the Lord. Show Him your gratitude.

Despite the mundane, everyday tasks we encounter, there is something special about each day. God has ordained that. He is in control. Praise and rejoice, for this *is* the day He has made (Psalm 118:24).

*Heavenly Father, I thank You for another day of life.
Let me celebrate this day and use it according to Your plan.*

PERSONAL CHOICE

*Truly no man can ransom another, or give to God the price of his life,
for the ransom of their life is costly and can never suffice.*
PSALM 49:7–8 ESV

There are some things no person can do for another. For example, none of us can make a decision to accept Christ for another. Every soul makes its own choice.

That truth hurts many of us because we love people who have resisted the Gospel message. Though we seek to share the joys of Jesus, some will never come to Him.

God does not hold us accountable for another's decision. He only tells us to bear the news. We should do that gently, with respect, because we all know those who have irritated others by coming on too strong. Pushing doesn't work. It causes resentment, not faith.

If a loved one refuses God, perhaps it's time to stop talking and start praying. Maybe another messenger will open that hard heart to the truth. Perhaps it's time to *live* our faith as much as speaking it.

Ultimately, that decision lies between one person and God. Give them the truth, let your loved ones choose, and trust God for the outcome.

*Lord, help me to share Your love with others in an attractive way.
You say each must make the choice. Help me to be fervent in prayer.*

WELL-AGED WISDOM

Hearken unto thy father that begat thee,
and despise not thy mother when she is old.
PROVERBS 23:22 KJV

Our culture seems allergic to age. Book, movie, and television plots rarely portray heroes and heroines above the age of thirty. Advertisements avoid older actors unless the product involves disease. Instead, the media presents young, healthy people as experts in every situation despite their lack of experience.

It's easy for Christians to absorb this attitude, especially when aged parents need help in managing their everyday lives. God does not expect us to agree with them all the time. The years take a toll on decision-making abilities, and sometimes we must make unpopular choices for our parents. But as we provide medical, financial, and household assistance, we should offer them as much independence as possible.

The Bible also urges younger believers to look to older Christians for advice and prayer. An eighty-five-year-old saint may use a walker, but the lifetime lessons of faith she has learned remain strong and steady. Her prayers for her children are no less powerful than when she prayed at their bedside; in fact, they have grown up with her sons, daughters, and grandchildren. An old man may seem at the mercy of his hearing aids, but his spiritual ears have sharpened with the years. He hears God clearly, and God always hears him.

Shouldn't we listen as well?

Father, You are the Ancient of Days. Help us to welcome
the wisdom You share with Your people, old and young.

....

....

....

....

....

....

OVERWHELMED? CRY OUT

[Prayer of the afflicted, when he is overwhelmed,
and poureth out his complaint before the Lord.]
Hear my prayer, O Lord, and let my cry come unto thee.
PSALM 102:1 KJV

If any word describes life in the twenty-first century, it's *overwhelming.*

It doesn't matter if we are single or married or if we stay home or have an outside job. Even with all of our modern conveniences, we never seem to get on top of things.

There's always one more thing to do; always one more hug to give, one more call to answer, one more crisis to solve.

Life never lets up.

It's overwhelming.

And it becomes more overwhelming when we get so busy that we forget our Source of strength and sanity. When we forget to pray.

May we never overlook this vital connection with God!

Our Lord loves us. He is not surprised when we are overwhelmed; He is not afraid of our complaints. He is ready to answer when we cry out for mercy and strength.

While God hears silent prayers, it is the cry of His people that seems to get the ear of God and move His hand more dramatically. When we cry out, we admit that we cannot help ourselves and that we need His help.

God is there. And He does not want us to be silent.

Father, HELP! I have more than I can handle. Help me to say yes to the best things
and no to those less important things that tend to overwhelm me. Thank You for
hearing my complaint and answering, for turning my plea into praise!

WHITE OR WHOLE WHEAT?

*You shall love the LORD your God with all your
heart and with all your soul and with all your might.*
DEUTERONOMY 6:5 ESV

Nutrition experts tell us to eat whole-grain breads because they're better for us. While white bread tastes good and is often easier to chew, it doesn't carry the whole-wheat loaf's nutrition.

Eating white bread is the physical version of loving God with only part of our hearts. Spiritually, we need the sustenance of a wholehearted faith; a deep, fruitful commitment that encompasses all our lives. We need to feed our minds with the Word, our hearts with an intimate relationship with Christ, and our spirits with prayer.

God is most gracious. He understands when responsibilities keep us from church—and He doesn't look poorly upon us. But that doesn't mean our faith life should die out entirely. Can we reprioritize a few things and go to an evening service? We need to meet with God's people. If that is utterly impossible, do we make the most of other methods that feed our souls?

Life can be a school of faith, but are we supporting it by fellowship with the saints? Let's not live white-bread lives when we can enjoy whole wheat.

*Lord, help me to love You with all my heart
and do all I can to get spiritual nutrition.*

STRESSED OUT?

God, the one and only—I'll wait as long as he says. Everything I need comes from him, so why not? He's solid rock under my feet, breathing room for my soul, an impregnable castle: I'm set for life.

PSALM 62:1 MSG

In our modern day, we invite stress into our lives. Busy schedules, financial strains, being overburdened with caring—it all adds up.

How do we handle the inevitable stress? Just let it go. Relinquish control to a loving God and realize that the reins are in His hands.

Give up control? we might think. *Isn't that dangerous?*

When we give our lives to Christ and accept His will—instead of vainly seeking to impose our own—we discover an inner peace. We can rest assured that His plans are the best. God is omnipotent, full of love, grace, and mercy. He knows what is best for us. His eyes roam the future He's planned for us.

Elisabeth Elliot said, "If my life is surrendered to God, all is well. Let me not grab it back as though it were in peril in His hand but would be safer in mine." Let go. Trust. Be less stressed.

Dear Jesus, it sounds so simple: let go. But it isn't. Help me trust in You and recognize that You're in control. I thank You for the plan You've established for my life.

24/7

He will not allow your foot to be moved;
He who keeps you will not slumber.
PSALM 121:3 NKJV

Are you old enough to remember when most stores were *not* "open twenty-four hours"? If you needed something but the store was closed, you just had to wait.

Some of the hardest waiting comes with medical or health issues: waiting for a surgery to be over, waiting for a chemo treatment to end, or waiting for a doctor to show up. Waiting to see a specialist, get into the lab, or experience the effects of a new medicine. It's easy to become discouraged when it seems that nothing we need is immediately accessible.

God, however, is always available. He doesn't hang out a CLOSED sign. He doesn't work a nine-to-five day then go off to do whatever He wants. With confidence, we can call on Him and know that He's listening.

Jesus showed us real accessibility: people came to Him during the day, at night, while he was eating, and when He was on His way to help someone else. A convicted criminal even called upon Jesus while they both hung on crosses.

The expression "24/7" is relatively new—but it describes perfectly how God takes care of us.

Gracious God, I'm so thankful I can come to You at any time
of the day or night and know that You're there.

GENEROUS SOWING

Remember this: Whoever sows sparingly will also reap sparingly,
and whoever sows generously will also reap generously.
2 CORINTHIANS 9:6 NIV

The concept of sowing and reaping is pretty simple. If you want a garden filled with colorful flowers, you start by planting seeds. If you want a large, fruitful garden, you've got to sow lots of seeds!

Blooming flowers attract people with their colorful petals and fragrant aromas. Well-kept gardens draw us in with their tasty variety of fruits and vegetables. Do you want to attract others to yourself and the God you serve? Want them to recognize the "fruit of the Spirit" residing in you? Want to win them with your fragrant aroma? Then sow seeds!

What seeds have you planted today? Kindness? Joy? Gentleness? Self-control? Goodness? If you drop those seeds into fertile soil—and what soil is more prepared than those you care for on a daily basis?—God will cause them to spring to life.

As you begin each day, ask the Lord to show you which seeds to plant. . .and how. Follow His lead. Then watch the blossoms of a fruitful life spring forth!

Heavenly Father, I want to bear fruit in my life. I want others to be drawn to
me so that I can effectively minister to them. Please help me to plant good seeds.
Show me when and where to do the planting so that the harvest will be plentiful!

FOREVER LOVE

Can anything ever separate us from Christ's love? Does it mean he no longer loves us if we have trouble or calamity, or are persecuted, or hungry, or destitute, or in danger, or threatened with death?

ROMANS 8:35 NLT

What does it take to make you doubt God's love for you? Financial difficulties, poor health, or job loss? A sick child, Alzheimer's, or cancer? The death of a parent, spouse, or child?

In Romans 8:28 Paul declares that God makes all these things work for our good because He uses them to mold us into the image of His Son. But when we experience these things, it can feel as though God has forgotten us. Satan would have us believe that God withdraws His love from us in order to punish us. So we draw back from loving Him; we build walls against the hurt of rejection and betrayal.

But God never promised to keep us or our loved ones from trouble. He loves us with an everlasting love. We are never out of His thoughts. He has engraved our names on His heart and His hand. In our trouble, God reveals Himself.

In *My Utmost for His Highest*, Oswald Chambers said, "Either Jesus Christ is a deceiver and Paul is deluded, or some extraordinary thing happens to a man who holds on to the love of God when the odds are all against God's character. . . . Only one thing can account for it—the love of God in Christ Jesus."

Father, may my love for You grow stronger in the trials,
knowing that Your love never fails.

THE "WAIT" ROOM

God, the one and only—I'll wait as long as he says.
Everything I hope for comes from him, so why not?
PSALM 62:5 MSG

Waiting doesn't fit today's immediate-results world. Technology and time-saving gadgets have conditioned us to be impatient people. We rush from place to place, from appointment to appointment. We fidget when we find a line blocking us from our goal or when the stoplight is red for more than a couple of minutes or when the preacher goes on "too long" with his sermon.

Yet much of life is learning to wait. The dictionary defines *waiting* as a time of stillness with an attitude of readiness or expectancy. Some Bible versions translate *waiting* as "resting."

God's timetable cannot be rushed. He is not bound by time nor does He run on man's schedule. So He gives us warm-up exercises of short waits or delays in our schedules—a light that stays red longer than we think it should or lines at the bank, grocery store, or pharmacy—to prepare us for the more intense times of life, such as wait times at the doctor's office and at hospital testing rooms or beside a loved one's deathbed. These are the times He calls us to rest in His time schedule, not anxious of the outcome, not striving for our own way, agenda, or deadline.

Take advantage of the "wait" training God has for you today. He will reward you with so much more when you do.

Father, please help me wait on You today, resting in the knowledge
of who You are and knowing that Your plan, Your timetable, is perfect.

JUST GOD'S NAME

We praise you, God, we praise you,
for your Name is near; people tell of your wonderful deeds.
PSALM 75:1 NIV

We trust certain names. There are products with particular brand names we buy over and over. We rely upon a certain repair company that we know provides quality services. Someone shares a good report about her doctor, and we see if he's taking new patients. Hearing the name of an old friend brings a smile.

"What's in a name?" William Shakespeare asked. If it's a reliable, honest name, we know we can put our faith in that name. Hearing that name brings peace and hope. We are thankful that name is present whenever a need arises.

Sometimes the reliable, honest name of God becomes a one-word prayer. We don't have the clarity or the energy to say much more. Just God's name.

We can't explain how we are feeling or what the next day will bring, so we call out His name. Just God's name.

The pain of grief may be so deep that repeating His name is our only comfort. Just God's name.

Friends and family may let us down, making us feel all alone. God's name goes with us through our dark times. Just God's name.

We can trust God's name. It's all we need. Just God's name.

Almighty God, I thank You for being near. You know what I need, and I trust You with my present and my future. You are my Lord, my God, and my Savior.

HAVE THE COMPASSION OF CHRIST

But when he saw the multitudes, he was moved with compassion on them, because they fainted, and were scattered abroad, as sheep having no shepherd.
MATTHEW 9:36 KJV

What's your day like today—busy?

In Matthew 9, Jesus was very busy. He healed a crippled man; invited a tax collector to be His disciple; gave a brief lecture on the new covenant; healed a woman, two blind men, and a demon-possessed man—and even raised a girl from the dead.

If we had been in Christ's sandals, we might have found a tree, sat down beneath it, and said, "Now that was good work—I did a good job today." But Jesus shows us that that's not enough.

After all He had done, He looked at the people and was "moved with compassion"—not because of their physical needs, but because they were spiritually lost.

If we serve others without directing them to the Good Shepherd who can save their souls, our service to them is in vain. And if we serve without compassion and love, we will not profit (1 Corinthians 13:3).

For fruit to abound, we must have the compassion of Christ that seeks to lead men and women to Him.

Father, let me see the true needs of those around me. Fill me with compassion for their souls. Use me to meet the greatest need in their lives—You.

KNEE MAIL

The prayer of a righteous person is powerful and effective.
JAMES 5:16 NIV

We've all had those inevitable days when we're exhausted or discouraged and it seems too hard to carry on. We feel as dry as the desert sand, with nothing left to give. This is a time when we could use nourishment for our souls.

The prophet Zechariah said, "Ask the LORD for rain in the spring, for he makes the storm clouds. And he will send showers of rain" (Zechariah 10:1 NLT). Commentator Matthew Henry explained this scripture by saying, "Spiritual blessings had been promised. . . . We must in our prayers ask for mercies in their proper time. The Lord would make bright clouds and give showers of rain. This may be an exhortation to seek the influences of the Holy Spirit, in faith and by prayer, through which the blessings held forth in the promises are obtained."

When these times occur, use "knee mail." Carve out some time to pray, to praise, and to petition our heavenly Father for the strength to carry on. He is faithful to answer our pleas and send refreshment to our hearts—maybe in the form of a restful night's sleep, a friend to encourage us, or a stranger's greeting.

We never know just how the Lord will answer our prayers, but answer He will. God's inbox is never too full.

Lord, how I long for Your presence. Father,
hear my prayers; extend Your hand of mercy to me.

SUCH AS WE HAVE

Then Peter said, Silver and gold have I none; but such as I have give I thee:
In the name of Jesus Christ of Nazareth rise up and walk.
ACTS 3:6 KJV

Our modern materialism often skews our spiritual thinking. When called upon to do a task, we often think we need to have all the money, equipment, and personnel we'll need in the end before we begin.

This is not God's methodology. God operates through us with "such as we have."

Peter and John didn't have money—but they did have the healing power of Jesus, which they offered in faith to the crippled man.

The little boy didn't have enough lunch to feed a multitude. But when he gave such as he had to Jesus, it multiplied.

The widow of Zarephath had only enough grain and oil for one meal, but she gave such as she had to Elijah, and she survived the famine.

When God gives us a job to do, He doesn't require our resources. He has everything He needs to accomplish His will. As Hudson Taylor said, "God's work done in God's way will never lack God's supply."

All God needs is such as we have—a willing heart and a willing body. He can—and will—take care of the rest.

Father, You have given me this task of caring for others, and it seems too big for me.
I don't have all the things I need to do the job. Yet I know that You do.
Father, I am willing to serve. Work through me as You desire.

HIDDEN THINGS

Call to me and I will answer you. I'll tell you marvelous and
wondrous things that you could never figure out on your own.
JEREMIAH 33:3 MSG

Life has a way of perplexing us. Just as we think we've got it all figured out, something happens to change everything. Chaos and confusion reign.

That's where Jeremiah found himself. God had called him to be His prophet to Israel. He gave him a specific message to preach. And Jeremiah obeyed when God promised to make him a strong tower against the evil that prevailed in the land.

Now Jeremiah is confined in the court of the guardhouse to the palace in Jerusalem. God's deliverance is seemingly nonexistent. Here God meets with Jeremiah and encourages him to pray for revelation. In a situation beyond Jeremiah's comprehension, God promises to reveal what has been previously hidden.

Again Jeremiah obeyed—though it made no sense—and God gave him a fresh vision of His purposes, far beyond what Jeremiah could have imagined.

God's promise holds true for us today. While we are only a small part of God's overall plan, He will reveal what we cannot see when we call on Him.

Father, I thank You that when I call on You, You answer. You reveal
Your way to me in terms that I can comprehend. One day I will
see the whole picture and marvel at Your wonderful ways.

STILL MY TROUBLED HEART

"Peace I leave with you; my peace I give you. I do not give to you as the world gives. Do not let your hearts be troubled and do not be afraid."
JOHN 14:27 NIV

We can call upon the Lord to give us peace: a peace that passes all understanding despite our circumstances. It's the same peace that calmed Peter on the open sea, Paul and Silas in prison, and Stephen as he faced martyrdom—the undeniable, indescribable calm from the Holy Spirit.

The peace that God extends to us can be accepted or ignored. In the frustrations of everyday life, it's entirely possible to turn our backs on this incredible gift—bringing on ourselves worry, stress, and loss of sleep. But accepting Jesus' gift of peace quiets our inner spirit and helps us to calm down.

When frets and worries assail, take a few moments to read the Bible. Turn to the psalms, read some out loud, and copy a line or two to stick in your pocket or on the bathroom mirror. Find words of praise penned by a man on the run: King David. He knew to pursue the heavenly Father for peace. We should do the same.

Father, please still my troubled heart. I need an extra
measure of peace this day. Thank You.

THE PRAYER MAP

Be joyful in hope, patient in affliction, faithful in prayer.
ROMANS 12:12 NIV

Did Paul get the cart before the horse here? No. But sometimes it helps to rearrange the words and ideas for a clearer look. We could paraphrase this verse as, "When we are faithful (and fervent) in prayer, we will become more joyful and patient in affliction."

It's easy to become so focused on particular situations or crises that we lose sight of God's ultimate purpose for us. We want to finish our tasks, return to our own agendas, and move on. But in His love, God keeps drawing our eyes and hearts back to a better destiny, a journey of the soul, a journey home.

Isn't *home* a beautiful word? It certainly is for God's children, whom Paul wrote to in Romans. Throughout his letter, he explains how Christians can, and do, reside in God's family by Christ's finished work on the cross. Then he calls them to abide in this family as faithful and fruitful sons and daughters.

Since affliction will come, he exhorts us all to faithful prayer, which always draws believers back to a sure hope—back to a trust in God's love and provision until the journey's end.

Father, as a believer, my ultimate destination is heaven. Keep me from grumbling when You have me take a bumpy side road rather than the interstate. Help me see how a rocky road may bring me closer to You.

THE SON IS SHINING

Then Jesus again spoke to them, saying, "I am the Light of the world;
he who follows Me will not walk in the darkness, but will have the Light of life."
JOHN 8:12 NASB

It is dark and dreary outside—and it seems that way inside, too. Everything feels cold and uncomfortable. It's hard just to get out of bed, let alone muster the energy to provide the care that God has called us to give.

But there is a bright light on the horizon! Jesus Christ, the Son, shines every day, regardless of the weather in our souls. Nothing can stop Him from shining—and He is waiting for us to come and bask in His light.

Jesus will brighten each day and give us the strength and energy to do His will. He will shine on us every minute, if only we'll ask Him to, and He can make what seems gloomy bright and full of His presence.

The Lord's light will shine in the darkness and cheer every corner of our world. The Son is shining in our lives today with a light that gives us the courage and strength to face any circumstance.

Thank You so much, Lord, that You are the spiritual Sun in my life—
and that You are there for me every single day. I praise Your holy name!

GETTING IT ALL DONE

But seek first his kingdom and his righteousness,
and all these things will be given to you as well.
MATTHEW 6:33 NIV

Have you ever thought of Jesus as a caregiver?

His disciples did—they followed Him everywhere and depended on Him for, well, everything. Then there were the sick people who constantly tugged at His robes and asked for healing. And there were those other people who came to Jesus for the healing of *others*. . . You get the idea.

Jesus definitely qualified as a caregiver. Even with all those demands, Jesus used His time perfectly. Not a moment was wasted. His Father approved of every single thing that He did. What was His secret? He shared it in Matthew 6:33: "Seek first his kingdom and his righteousness".

It seems miraculous that Jesus could find time to heal the sick, raise the dead, teach His disciples, feed hungry crowds, even enjoy a meal with friends on occasion. But He was able to do all that because He had His priorities in order. Always. God came first—God's kingdom, God's righteousness. This was the single most important priority in Jesus' ministry. Everything else followed.

What would your day look like if God came first? What would happen if you *only* did the things He wanted you to do? Give it a try—you'll be amazed at the results.

Jesus, I thank You for Your example as the perfect Caregiver. Teach me how
to put You first and to trust You with all that I need to accomplish.

BLIND SKIER

For this God is our God for ever and ever;
he will be our guide even to the end.
PSALM 48:14 NIV

Attached to each other by harnesses and a pole, a pair of skiers slid in tandem down a slope. The one in back wore a large orange sign that said, in black letters, BLIND SKIER. Zooming sightless down a snow-covered slope, he exuded personal courage and trust in his guide.

Sometimes life is that hill. Our path is steep, scary, and potentially dangerous.

We are the blind skier—our limitations prevent us from seeing or successfully weaving our way through the challenges of life.

But God is the front skier—expert, all-seeing, completely in charge, and totally caring. He carefully guides us through each day's obstacles. We can't see Him; we can only trust that He'll bring us through. On the brink of our "hills," we could sit down in the snow and refuse to budge, crying over our limitations, the scary circumstances, and the fact that we can't see God.

Or, using His Word as our harness and pole, we can securely follow Him down the hill. We can exercise courage and faith, clinging to His promise to safely maneuver us through the challenges ahead.

As you go about your day, remember that blind skier. Cling to the pole. Rest confidently in the harness, knowing that God is on the other side.

Lord, when I can't see You, when circumstances obscure Your goodness,
help me to remember Your Word to me. Enable me to follow
You closely through the frightening course of my life.

NO AFTERNOON PICNIC

Take everything the Master has set out for you, well-made weapons....
This is no afternoon athletic contest that we'll walk away from and
forget about in a couple of hours. This is for keeps, a life-or-death
fight to the finish against the Devil and all his angels.
EPHESIANS 6:11–12 MSG

The first major land battle of the American Civil War was fought near Manassas, Virginia, on July 21, 1861. Certain of a Union victory, many of the Washington DC elite rode out in their carriages to watch the battle. But with the Union soldiers untrained and undisciplined, the battle soon turned into a rout that had the Union forces scattering in retreat. The panicked civilians added to the confusion as they attempted to flee both armies.

We, too, are in a battle. Even though our opponent is invisible, this battle is no less real than any other fought in the many wars in the history of the world. It isn't an afternoon picnic in the park, complete with volleyball or softball, where we vie for athletic superiority. It's a lifelong fight to the death.

The only way to be successful against Satan and his evil forces is to take up the armor God has given us, utilizing the weapons of prayer and scripture in order to successfully parry the darts and sword thrusts the enemy sends our way. The battle is fierce even though the war is won.

Father, please give me wisdom, strength, and determination to stand
firm in the battle raging about me. Help me use all the armor
and weapons You have given me to their fullest extent.

SERVE WITH THE SOUL IN MIND

To the weak became I as weak, that I might gain the weak: I am
made all things to all men, that I might by all means save some.
1 CORINTHIANS 9:22 KJV

As an apostle, Paul had the right—and the power—to preach the Gospel with no holds barred. He could have thundered the Gospel from his pulpit without regard for the minds and hearts of those in his audience.

But that wasn't Paul's style. As a Jew, he reasoned with the Jews, showing them that the law was given to lead them to Christ. Using his great intellect, he reasoned with the Greeks at Mars Hill, declaring the true identity of their "UNKNOWN GOD" (Acts 17:23 KJV). Acknowledging his own weaknesses, he showed the weak the strength of Christ.

In other words, Paul met people where they were. He empathized and identified with them so they could see how Christ could work in their lives.

As we interact with those around us, we must know them as they are, without prejudice, so we can show them how Jesus can take them from their sinful state to His holy heaven.

Our goal is not to be honored for our sacrifices but to honor the Father by gaining the lost. Serve with the soul in mind, so that through you, God will save some.

Dear Jesus, please help me to understand the deep needs of the people
around me so I can show them how You can make a difference
in their lives. Please save some today.

BORROWING TROUBLE

Why are you down in the dumps, dear soul? Why are you crying the blues?
Fix my eyes on God—soon I'll be praising again. He puts a
smile on my face. He's my God.
PSALM 43:5 MSG

One evening a man found himself staggering alone under a burden heavy enough to crush a half dozen strong men. Out of sheer exhaustion he put down his entire load and took a good look at it. He found that it was all borrowed: part of it belonged to the following day; part of it belonged to the following week. Yet it was crushing him *now*.

Sound familiar? We often find ourselves carrying a load of responsibility, worry, and grief. Ignored, the burden soon grows too heavy to bear, robbing us of the joy of life.

Take a good look at your burden. Is it borrowed from tomorrow, next week, or even further down the road? Jesus said, "Do not worry about tomorrow, for tomorrow will worry about itself. Each day has enough trouble of its own" (Matthew 6:34 NIV).

Fix your eyes on God, the great burden-bearer. Roll all the care, the worry, the responsibility, and the grief on Him. Allow Him to manage every detail. He wants to put praise in your heart and a smile on your face.

Father, give me the wisdom not to borrow trouble from the future. When I trust You
to help me bear only today's problems, the load lifts and the praise begins.

GOD'S FORMULA FOR HAPPINESS

Is anyone among you in trouble? Let them pray.
Is anyone happy? Let them sing songs of praise.
JAMES 5:13 NIV

Humanity's formula for happiness is vastly different from God's. We most often live to please ourselves, and when things don't go our way, we grumble. The Lord wants us to live for Him. And whether we're happy or sad, He longs for us to lift our voices in praise.

So what *is* God's formula for happiness? Prayer and praise. Sounds simple, right? Not necessarily. Imagine that you're in the throes of caring for someone who doesn't seem to be improving. You've cried out to God, but silence on His end has you boggled. So you stop praying. You stop asking. You give up. Oh sure, you still offer up some basic, generic prayers. But praise? No way.

God longs for us to keep on knocking, keep on seeking. When you're going through rough times, slip into your prayer closet and spend time with your heavenly Father—praying *and* praising. When you're faced with times of silence from God, don't take it as apathy on His part. While you're waiting, continue in a hopeful mind-set of prayer and praise.

Lord, I don't like to wait. And it's hard for me to imagine praying and praising my way through a situation when I don't have the answer yet. Help me to learn Your formula for happiness. Teach me to wait patiently. . .hopefully.

FAITHFUL, NOT FAMOUS

The Lord give mercy unto the house of Onesiphorus;
for he oft refreshed me, and was not ashamed of my chain.
2 TIMOTHY 1:16 KJV

Onesiphorus is mentioned only twice in the Bible. Paul introduces him in his letter to Timothy as a person who went out of his way to refresh and encourage him—a sharp contrast to Phygellus and Hermogenes, who had deserted Paul (2 Timothy 1:15). We might view these fair-weather friends with scorn. But in that volatile political climate, those who associated with the apostle put themselves at risk. After all, the Romans had imprisoned Paul, and they often did not hesitate to jail a convict's friends.

Onesiphorus, however, did not let that stop him. He not only helped Paul nurture the fledgling church in Ephesus but determined to help and encourage his friend when the Romans imprisoned him. Onesiphorus went to Rome and searched the city until he tracked Paul down and met his needs.

While few Christians in North America languish in prisons because of persecution, many suffer from illnesses and old age, which distance them from the believing community. Fortunately, modern-day encouragers like Onesiphorus seek out these needy Christians with a refreshing ministry that blesses lonely, hurting hearts. Jesus, who commanded His followers to visit prisoners, honors those who serve shut-ins with love like His.

Lord Jesus, even though my contributions to Your kingdom seem insignificant,
You never forget a cup of cold water or a smile given in Your name. Thank You!

AT ROPE'S END

We were under great pressure, far beyond our ability to endure, so that we despaired of life itself. Indeed, we felt we had received the sentence of death. But this happened that we might not rely on ourselves but on God, who raises the dead. He has delivered us from such a deadly peril, and he will deliver us again. On him we have set our hope that he will continue to deliver us.

2 CORINTHIANS 1:8–10 NIV

Some people have said that when they reached the end of their rope, they tied a knot and hung on. Others have said that living through great difficulty showed them that they didn't know as much as they thought they did but that they were stronger than they imagined they were.

Still others say that God's children endure suffering until they realize that circumstances are far more difficult than they can handle. At that point, each person has a choice: curse God like Job's wife recommended, or embrace God like Job did. Who can forget Job's moving affirmation, "I know that my redeemer lives, and that in the end he will stand on the earth" (Job 19:25 NIV)?

When we focus intently on God rather than our difficult situations, He sustains and fills us with hope and joy—helping us to continue our journeys. Eventually, He delivers us. When we are saved, we know *who* saved us.

When you reach your rope's end, count on God. He will deliver you.

God, life is too much for me today. Help!

THE BLESSINGS TO COME

*You know that you will receive an inheritance from the Lord
as a reward. It is the Lord Christ you are serving.*
Colossians 3:24 NIV

Even city folk know that if we plant a kernel of corn, it produces several ears of corn, loaded with many more kernels. A single sunflower seed grows into a tall, sturdy stalk with a heavy golden head holding hundreds of seeds. It's amazing how great a return we get when we plant seeds in a garden or field.

We are sowing good things into other people's lives. It may sometimes seem like a thankless job, but God sees all that we do—and in time, He will reward us with a great "crop" for our efforts.

That's another thing about sowing seeds: they produce their fruit in a future season. A day or week after we sow, it looks like nothing is happening. But with the appropriate sun, rain, and time, tender plants rise up from the ground. As the weeks continue, the plants grow stronger, become fruitful, and produce a harvest.

Whenever we serve others, God rewards us. It may not be as quickly as we'd like— but it will certainly be good. We can count on the Lord!

*I am grateful, dear Lord, that You love me and notice the things
I do for others. Thank You for rewarding me—in Your time.*

SING A NEW SONG

Everything has happened just as I said it would.... Tell the whole world to sing a new song to the LORD!... Join in the praise.
ISAIAH 42:9-10 CEV

Jeremiah loved his people, but the message God called him to preach was a harsh one—judgment was coming. Along with God's call to Jeremiah came a caveat: "I have put My words in your mouth. But, Jeremiah, they're not going to listen to you. In fact, they are going to persecute you, punish you, and even try to kill you. But you continue to speak My words to them, and I will protect you and deliver you."

When the high priest, Pashhur, heard Jeremiah preach against Judah's sin and proclaim the coming judgment, he put Jeremiah in the stocks. But as soon as Pashhur released him, Jeremiah spoke judgment against Pashhur himself (Jeremiah 20).

Later, Jeremiah complained to God that every time he opened his mouth to speak His word, he was made a laughingstock, a mockery to his people. His obedience resulted in reproach and derision. But in the midst of his complaint, Jeremiah burst forth in a song of praise to God for delivering him from the hands of his persecutors.

When you are misunderstood and your motives are questioned, sing to the Lord a new song of deliverance and praise. He will deliver His people no matter how impossible the circumstances are.

Father, I lift up my song of praise to You today,
for You alone can deliver me from the enemy's clutches.

DEEDS OF WISDOM

Who is wise and understanding among you? Let them show it by their good life, by deeds done in the humility that comes from wisdom.
JAMES 3:13 NIV

Have you ever met someone who seems to have the gift of "understanding"? Such a person is genuinely compassionate because they relate to other people. They connect on a deep level.

How much more wonderful would it be if we walked in understanding with God, especially during the tough seasons of our lives? We would think His thoughts, have His heart for people, act the way He acts, and respond the way He responds. In short, we would be His hands and feet in action.

If you're struggling to have genuine compassion, if you're trying your best to make something work that doesn't seem to, ask God to give you His kind of understanding. Once you catch a glimpse of His heart for another person, then your deeds will arise from a place of godly sincerity. And those deeds, which spring from your relationship with Him, will be evident to everyone you come in contact with.

Dear Lord, I want to genuinely care for those You've entrusted to me. Not just tolerate them. Not just serve them. Give me Your understanding, and motivate me to act—and react—only as You would.

SECRET PETITIONS

Take delight in the LORD, and he will give you the desires of your heart.
PSALM 37:4 NIV

We all have them. Things that are so dear to us we can't share them with others. Feelings and desires that we don't want to reveal for fear of being judged insensitive, unloving, selfish, or ambitious.

Only God knows these desires. In many cases He's the One who has placed them in our hearts. The longing to see our loved ones well, happy, and fulfilled. Knowing God and following Him completely. The longing to be freed of certain responsibilities because they are hard to bear.

When we find ourselves in circumstances not of our own making and opposite of what we expected from the realization of our desires and dreams, it's easy to turn away from God. Yet we're told to *delight* in Him—to take joy in the circumstances in which we find ourselves, to rejoice in every situation, to praise Him because He is good and faithful and loving.

Delight in the knowledge that He is proving Himself to you as you deal with that special-needs child or dependent parent or spouse. Delight in knowing that God's love never fails, His grace is always sufficient, and His presence is always near. He will grant us our deepest desires in ways we don't expect.

Father, remind me to focus on You—on Your characteristics and attributes—
as I walk the path You have set before me. Help me to experience Your
love and grace, Your strength and wisdom, as I need them today.

HOPE

Why, my soul, are you downcast? Why so disturbed within me?
Put your hope in God, for I will yet praise him, my Savior and my God.
PSALM 42:5–6 NIV

If you've ever been depressed, you're not alone. Depression can be caused by circumstances, biology, environment, or a combination of all of those things. Research indicates that as many as 25 percent of Americans suffer from depression at some point in their lives.

We are blessed with scriptural accounts of godly people like David and Jeremiah, who struggled with depression. These stories let us know that it's a normal human reaction to feel overcome by the difficulties of life.

While feeling this way is normal, it doesn't have to be the norm. As Christians, we have hope. Hope that our circumstances will not always be the way they are right now. Hope that no matter how dismal the world situation seems to be, God wins in the end. Hope that eternity is just on the other side.

Hope is like a little green shoot poking up through hard, cracked ground. When you're depressed, do what David and Jeremiah did—pour out your heart to God. Seek help from a trusted friend or godly counselor.

Look for hope. It's all around you, and it's yours for the taking.

Father, even when I am depressed, You are still God. Help me to find
a ray of hope in the midst of dark circumstances. Amen.

FEAR-FREE

You will not fear the terror of night, nor the arrow that flies by day.
PSALM 91:5 NIV

Were you afraid of the dark when you were a little girl? It's hard to be comfortable when you can't see what's out there, right? Even as a big girl, the nighttime hours can still be a little scary. Seems like we're most vulnerable to fears and failures in the wee hours, when the darkness closes in around us.

So how do you face the "terror of night" without fear? You have to grasp the reality that God is bigger and greater than anything that might evoke fear. He's bigger than financial struggles. He's bigger than job stress. He's even bigger than relational problems. Best of all, He can see in the dark. He knows what's out there and can deal with it. All it takes is one sentence from Him—*Let there be light!*—and darkness dispels.

We serve an awesome and mighty God, One who longs to convince us He's mighty enough to save us even when the darkness seeps in around us. So don't fear what you can't see. Or what you *can* see. Hand over that fear and watch God-ordained faith rise up in its place.

Father, I'm glad You can see in the dark. Sometimes I face the unseen things of my life with fear gripping my heart. I release that fear to You today. Thank You for replacing it with godly courage.

MY THIRSTY SOUL

*You, God, are my God, earnestly I seek you; I thirst for you, my whole being
longs for you, in a dry and parched land where there is no water.*
PSALM 63:1 NIV

Let's face it—life provides us little leisure time. Days slip away from us until we find
ourselves falling exhausted into bed—often without having spent any time with the
Lord. But our connection with God through prayer and Bible study is an absolute
necessity.

God doesn't expect us to spend three hours a day in intense prayer or devote an
entire evening to an in-depth study of the Bible's original Hebrew and Greek words.
But He does ask for a little of the time we have. If the only "alone moments" we can
offer Him are during our drive time to work, He'll take them!

Finding quiet time with God is crucial for our spiritual, mental, even physical
health. Let's think of our alone time with Him as a period of refreshing for whatever
strength, wisdom, or encouragement we'll need to succeed in the day before us.

The psalmist describes a "dry and parched land," ready to absorb an evening rain
or morning dew. What a picture of our lives, eagerly awaiting our Lord's life-giving
sustenance.

*Lord, though I truly need You, I'm not always quick to recognize that truth.
Cause me to see that You alone meet my deepest needs. Then shower me
with Your living water and refresh my spirit until my cup overflows.*

TIME CLOCKS

Is not the LORD your God with you?
and hath he not given you rest on every side?
1 CHRONICLES 22:18 KJV

The time clock is a wonderful invention. You clock in and (here is the best part) you clock out! While we're "on the clock," we're aware that our time is not our own. Whether cooking for a hungry throng of customers, typing on a keyboard, or emptying trash, for a set time we must do another's bidding. Then we go home, off the clock at last.

At home, there is no time clock. No way to "punch out" for the day. Our duties seem endless: picking up dry cleaning, rushing to a soccer game, folding the millionth load of laundry, trying to find an interesting way to use hamburger *again*, reading to the kids, helping with homework. . . Where's the time clock to put an end to this work?

God promises to give His people rest. The laundry will be there tomorrow. We can occasionally live with cereal for dinner. The vacuuming can wait for the weekend. Algebra will always be hard.

Slow down. Rest. Catch your breath. Allow God to renew you. You have His permission to clock out for the day.

Father God, teach me how to slow down. There are so many pressing needs,
yet I know I must find a way to clock out for the day. Enable me to rest in You.

CHRIST, MY IDENTITY

The LORD your God is with you, the Mighty Warrior who saves. He will take
great delight in you; in his love he will no longer rebuke you,
but will rejoice over you with singing.
ZEPHANIAH 3:17 NIV

As women, we love to love. We tend to trust easily. If we are married, we expect our husbands to look after our children and us, to admire and desire us as wives, to always be our protectors. Even if we've never been married, most of us have dreamed of such a relationship.

But when our expectations fall short and we find ourselves parenting alone—whatever the reason—our spirits shatter into a million little pieces. Often, we lose our identity. Any self-esteem we may once have had evaporates along with our dreams.

But God Himself, the maker of all creation, the very One who hung the stars in space and calls them by name, looks at each one of us with love. In His eyes are delight and joy. Because the Father has created us in His own image, He knows every hurt we feel—and He will quiet us with His love. He rejoices that we are His daughters, and He delights in us—not because of anything we do but simply because we are His.

Lord Jesus, though I sometimes feel alone and without an identity, I trust that
You are with me. I ask that You will quiet my spirit with Your mighty
peace and allow me to know the depth of Your love for me.

HURT BY OTHERS' CHOICES

God heard the boy crying. The angel of God called from Heaven to Hagar,
"What's wrong, Hagar? Don't be afraid. God has heard
the boy and knows the fix he's in."
GENESIS 21:17 MSG

A slave during early biblical times, Hagar had little say in her life decisions—others made them for her. Because of the infertility of her mistress, Sarah, Hagar became the concubine of Sarah's husband, Abraham, and gave birth to Ishmael.

At first, Hagar's hopes soared. Her son would become Abraham's heir, rich and powerful beyond her wildest dreams! However, the surprise appearance of Isaac, the late-life son of Sarah and Abraham, destroyed Hagar's fantasies of a wonderful future. Sarah wanted Hagar and Ishmael out of their lives. Abraham, though upset, loaded Hagar with water and food and told her to take Ishmael into the unforgiving desert.

When their water supply failed, Hagar laid her dehydrated son under a bush and walked away crying because she could not bear to watch Ishmael die. But God showed Hagar a well of water. Quickly she gave her child a drink. Both survived, and "God was on the boy's side as he grew up" (Genesis 21:20 MSG).

God is also on our side when we suffer because of others' choices. Even when we have lost hope, God's plan provides a way for us and those we love.

Heavenly Father, when my world seems out of control,
please help me love and trust You—even in the deserts of life.

COMMITMENT CHALLENGES AT CHURCH

Remember me for this, my God, and do not blot out what I have so faithfully done for the house of my God and its services.

NEHEMIAH 13:14 NIV

Have you ever sacrificed precious "leisure" hours to serve on a church committee, count offerings, or weed church flower beds? Despite your work schedule and double duty at home, you agree to co-teach Bible school—only to receive a phone call the night before from your partner. She has decided to go on vacation instead! Now, surrounded by hyper kindergarteners, you wonder what you did to deserve this.

Nehemiah felt the same way. A governor during Old Testament times, he spearheaded the rebuilding of Jerusalem's broken walls, then spent years encouraging his countrymen to worship Yahweh. He organized priests and Levites and served as a spiritual lay leader. He managed the practical affairs of the temple, including schedules, payments, and distributions. Nehemiah fought enemies, settled internal squabbles, and—and—*and!* His days never seemed long enough. He grew discouraged when trusted fellow workers in God's house placed their priorities elsewhere. Between crises, Nehemiah took a deep breath and prayed the above prayer.

More than twenty-five hundred years later, God tells the story of Nehemiah's perseverance in the Bible. Like you, Nehemiah may not have seen his reward as soon as he wanted. But now he is enjoying it forever.

So will you.

Lord Jesus, when I feel tired and unappreciated as I serve others, let Your applause be enough for me.

CLAP YOUR HANDS!

Clap your hands, all you nations; shout to God with cries of joy. For the LORD Most High is awesome, the great King over all the earth. . . . God has ascended amid shouts of joy, the LORD amid the sounding of trumpets. Sing praises to God, sing praises; sing praises to our King, sing praises.
PSALM 47:1–2, 5–6 NIV

In 1931, German theologian Dietrich Bonhoeffer spent a year at a seminary in New York City. While there, he was introduced to a church in Harlem. Astounded, then delighted, at the emotion expressed in worship, he returned to Germany with recordings of Gospel music tucked in his suitcase. Bonhoeffer knew that the worship he observed was authentic and pleasing to God.

King David would have loved Gospel music! Many of the psalms were meant to be sung loudly and joyfully. David appointed four thousand professional musicians—playing cymbals, trumpets, rams' horns, tambourines, harps, and lyres—for temple worship. We can imagine they would have rocked the roofs off of our modern-day church services!

Dancing was a part of worship in David's day, too. David angered his wife, Michal, with his spontaneous dance in the street as the ark of the covenant was returned to Jerusalem (1 Chronicles 15:29). The world, in David's viewpoint, couldn't contain the delight that God inspires. Neither could he!

How often do we worship God with our whole hearts? Do we ever burst forth in a song of praise? Do we clap our hands and lift them up high? Probably not often enough. Let's try that today!

O Lord, great is Your name and worthy of praise!

GOD'S MIRROR

Charm is deceptive, and beauty does not last; but a woman who fears the LORD will be greatly praised.
PROVERBS 31:30 NLT

A woman admitted that she spent much of her attention on how she looked and who was looking at her. She even watched her reflection in store windows to see how passersby reacted as she walked down the street.

Her overwhelming focus on appearance was driven by a fear of being alone. The woman was afraid that if she wasn't outwardly attractive, she might never find a husband. But she misunderstood what really determined her value.

Proverbs 31:30 shares a very important truth about charm and beauty: they fade. If a woman marries primarily on the basis of physical beauty, the couple will eventually be left wanting. Much more fulfilling to a marriage is the woman's spiritual focus.

May our minds be focused on the qualities that last: honesty, faithfulness, loyalty, and spiritual growth. Mr. Right will define beauty as God does—and will value good personal qualities above physical perfection.

Today, gaze into the mirror of scripture. Allow your true beauty to be that inner beauty of the soul—a reflection of Christ—that never fades.

Father, thank You for the beauty that You reflect from my soul. Help me to place less importance on my outward appearance and more value on the inner qualities that You are developing in me.

IDEAL PLACE

For consider your calling, brethren, that there were not many wise according to the flesh, not many mighty, not many noble; but God has chosen the foolish things of the world.

1 CORINTHIANS 1:26–27 NASB

Once my life is running smoothly. . .
  If I didn't have toddlers underfoot. . .
  As soon as I get this anger problem under control. . .
  When I get enough money. . .
  As soon as I (fill in the blank). . .then I can be used by God.

We are *where* we are *when* we are because our Father chose us for such a time as this. Our steps are ordered by Him. Whether He has called us to teach a Sunday school class, pray with other moms, lead a Bible study, or sing in the choir—we need not wait for the ideal time and place to serve Him. The only "ideal" is where you are right now.

God delights in using His people—right in the middle of all that appears crazy and wrong and hopeless. *Now* is the time to serve God, not next week or next year or when things get better. He wants our cheerful, obedient service right in the midst of—even in spite of—our difficult circumstances.

Father, help me see that there is no "ideal" place or circumstance to serve You. You can, and will, use me right where I am. Thank You that I do not have to have it all together to be used by You.

GOD IN THE DETAILS

When we heard of it, our hearts melted in fear and everyone's
courage failed because of you, for the LORD your God is
God in heaven above and on the earth below.
JOSHUA 2:11 NIV

The people of Jericho had reason to be worried. They had seen evidence of God's strength and support of His children—and knew that Joshua planned to conquer Canaan. As residents of the key military fortress in the land, they understood that Joshua would soon be at their gates.

Yet only Rahab seemed to recognize the right course of action: to embrace the Lord and open her home to Joshua's agents. In return, they made sure she and her family survived the attack. Because of her courage and faith, Rahab became an ancestor of Jesus.

Sometimes, when our own lives seem to be under siege from the demands of work, bills, and other worries, finding the work of God amid the strife can be difficult. Even though we acknowledge His power, we may overlook the gentle touches, the small ways in which He makes every day a little easier. Just as the Lord cares for the tiniest bird (Matthew 10:29–31), so He seeks to be a part of every detail in your life. Look for Him there.

Father God, I know You are by my side every day, good or bad,
and that You love and care for me. Help me to see Your
work in my life and in the lives of those around me.

BUDGET BREAKER

*Then the LORD said to Moses, "Behold, I will rain bread from heaven for you;
and the people shall go out and gather a day's portion every day,
that I may test them, whether or not they will walk in My instruction."*
EXODUS 16:4 NASB

The month lasted longer than the paycheck. The grocery bill exceeded the budget. Childcare expenses surpassed the rent. It's not an easy road to travel, yet one that many of us walk.

Isn't it interesting that we can trust God for eternal life, yet find it harder to trust Him for help with the mortgage?

In the Old Testament, God told the wandering Israelites He would feed them "manna from heaven," but with one caveat: He would only allow them to gather enough food for one day. No storing food away for the dreaded "what-ifs" of tomorrow. They would simply have to trust their God to faithfully supply their needs.

They didn't always past the "trust test"—and neither do we. But thankfully, God is faithful in spite of us! He will meet our needs when we come to Him in simple trust. Then we can bask in His faithfulness.

*Father, Your Word promises to supply all my needs. I trust You in spite
of the challenges I see. You are ever faithful. Thank You!*

PERFECT PRAYERS

This, then, is how you should pray: . . .
MATTHEW 6:9 NIV

How many messages have you heard on prayer? Have you ever come away thinking, *Did you hear how eloquently they prayed? How spiritual they sounded? No wonder God answers their prayers!*

Sometimes we take the straightforward and uncomplicated idea of prayer—the simple give-and-take of talking with God—and turn it into something hard. How many times have we made it a mere religious exercise, performed best by the "holy elite," rather than what it really is—conversation with God our Father.

Just pour out your heart to God. Share how your day went. Tell Him your dreams. Ask Him to search you and reveal areas of compromise. Thank Him for your lunch. Plead for your kids' well-being. Complain about your car. . . . Just talk with Him. Don't worry how impressive (or unimpressive!) you sound.

Talk with God while doing dishes, driving the car, folding laundry, eating lunch, or kneeling by your bed. Whenever, wherever, whatever—tell Him. He cares!

Don't allow this day to slip away without talking to your Father. No perfection required.

Father God, what a privilege it is to unburden my heart to You.
Teach me the beauty and simplicity of simply sharing my day with You.

SMILES BRING JOY

Light in a messenger's eyes brings joy to the heart,
and good news gives health to the bones.
PROVERBS 15:30 NIV

The teenage girl nervously walked backstage. It was her turn next. She had practiced for hours. This song was perfect, her teacher had said. But the butterflies in her stomach were telling a different story. Fear began to grip her throat. She couldn't breathe. It was then that she saw her mother sitting in the front row. There she was, eyes sparkling, smiling that goofy smile and proudly saying, "My daughter is next! She is so talented!" The young girl took a deep breath and closed her eyes. The fear melted and confidence took over. *I can do this*, she thought as she boldly walked onstage.

Smiles can say so many things in a quiet, gentle form. They can give comfort and support and bring joy and strength to someone who is weary. Courage and confidence are given by the love that smiles portray. They can simply remind a person that someone really does care. And more often than not, a smile is immediately returned to the giver.

Joy is contagious; spread it around. Smile at someone today. Go ahead and chuckle at that joke. Laugh with someone. Not only will you be blessing another, but you will be blessed yourself.

Dear Lord, fill me with Your joy today that I may bless others with my smile
and laughter and portray Your love to those around me. Amen.

JESUS' WRISTWATCH

Be very careful, then, how you live—not as unwise but as wise,
making the most of every opportunity, because the days are evil.
EPHESIANS 5:15–16 NIV

Time is money, they say. Society preaches the value of making good use of our time—and the expense of wasting it.

In the Bible, Ephesians 5 speaks of using every opportunity wisely. But even though scripture teaches the value of time, Jesus never wore a watch. He didn't view His opportunities within the bounds of earthly time.

Have you ever ended a day with guilt and regret over the growing black hole of work yet to be completed? Or do you feel peace at the end of your day, having walked in the presence of the Lord?

Satan wants to consume you with endless lists of meaningless tasks. Fight back! Concern yourself less with the items you can cross off your to-do list and more with those things the Lord would have you spend your time and energy on. You can strive to be a great multitasker or workhorse—but it's more important and fulfilling to be an efficient laborer for the Lord.

Father, help me to see where You are working and join You there. Let me place
my list of tasks aside as I seek Your will for me today. Then give me
the ability to show myself grace over the things I do not get done.

TWO HOPELESS SISTERS

Lot and his two daughters left Zoar and settled in the mountains, for he was afraid to stay in Zoar. He and his two daughters lived in a cave. One day the older daughter said to the younger, "Our father is old, and there is no man around here to give us children, as is the custom all over the earth."
GENESIS 19:30–31 NIV

Those poor sisters. These girls had been raised in Sodom, a Canaanite city so corrupt that God sent angels to destroy it. Lot fled with his daughters and lived in a cave.

In that primitive culture, hope for a secure future rested entirely on a son's shoulders. Lot's daughters were out of luck. There were no bachelors hanging around the caves. Desperate, hopeless, and faithless, the daughters came up with an idea: get their father drunk, then sleep with him to conceive a child.

It's hard to feel anything but disgust for those two sisters. But how many times have we scrambled to find a man- (or woman-)made answer to our problems? How many times have we turned to God as an afterthought?

The Lord is faithful even when we are not. Scripture tells us that the older daughter had a son named Moab, father of the Moabites. Five hundred years later, a Moabite baby grew up to become Ruth, grandmother of Israel's great King David.

Heavenly Father, when will I learn to turn to You to solve my problems? When I go my own way, it ends in disaster. Thank You that even my poor choices are not beyond Your ability to redeem.

ONE THING IS NEEDED

"Martha, Martha," the Lord answered, "you are worried and
upset about many things, but few things are needed—or indeed only one."
LUKE 10:41-42 NIV

We are each given twenty-four hours in a day. Einstein and Edison were given no more than Joseph and Jeremiah of the Old Testament. The president and the paratrooper are all given an equal share. Even Mother Teresa and plain ol' moms are peers when it comes to time.

Time—we can't buy it, save it, or get a greater share no matter what we do. Its value is beyond measure. So we should learn to use it carefully. Do we tackle the laundry now or help the kids read *If You Give a Mouse a Cookie* one more time? Do we stay up late, cleaning the living room, or slip into bed early, knowing we need the rest? Do we fuss over our hair and makeup or find a moment to kneel before our Father?

Since God has blessed each of us with twenty-four hours, let's seek His direction on how to spend this invaluable commodity wisely, giving more to people than things, spending more time on relationships than the rat race. In Luke, our Lord reminded dear, dogged, drained Martha that only one thing is needed—Him.

Father God, oftentimes I get caught up in the minutia of life. The piled laundry
can appear more important than the precious little ones You've given me.
Help me to use my time wisely. Open my eyes to see what is truly important.

LADIES IN WAITING

I will wait for the LORD. . . . I will put my trust in him.
ISAIAH 8:17 NIV

Modern humans aren't good at waiting. In our fast-paced society, if you can't keep up, you'd better get out of the way. We have fast food, speed dialing, and jam-packed schedules that are impossible to keep. Instant gratification is the name of the game—and that attitude often affects us.

The Lord Jesus Christ doesn't care about instant gratification. Our right-now attitudes don't move Him. Maybe He finds the saying, "Give me patience, Lord, *right now,*" humorous—but He rarely answers that particular prayer.

Do we want joy without accepting heartache? Peace without living through the stress? Patience without facing demands? God sees things differently. He's giving us the opportunity to learn through these delays, irritations, and struggles. What a wise God He is!

We especially need to learn the art of waiting on God. He will come through every time—but in *His* time, not ours. The wait may be hours or days—or it could be years. But God is always faithful to provide for us. It is when we learn to wait on Him that we will find joy, peace, and patience through the struggle.

Father, You know what I need, so I will wait. Help me be patient, knowing that You control my situation and that all good things come in Your time.

BLESSING, NOT BLASTING

Bless the LORD, O my soul: and all that is within me, bless his holy name.
PSALM 103:1 KJV

Many people in our country claim they do not believe in God; others shrug and say they don't know if He exists. But whenever a copier jams at work, or a dish is dropped in a restaurant, or a flight is delayed, atheists and agnostics include God in the midst of their misery. They yell His name as if *He* messed up on the job—even though they believe He doesn't officially exist.

We as Christians are called to invest all our emotional energy in blessing God rather than blasting Him. When others demean their day as "god-awful," we can choose to experience a "God-wonderful" day. When others swear at traffic, we can sing praises along with a CD or the radio. With His help—because no one can praise God without tapping into the power of His Spirit—we can develop spiritual radar that detects daily God-moments worthy of applause: rainbows and roses, clean water to drink, and belly laughs with our kids.

Every day God stacks His gifts around us as if it were Christmas. Like children, we can't give Him much. But we can offer all we are to bless His holy name. And that's the present He loves most.

Lord, each day I encounter thousands of opportunities to bless You, the Lord of the universe. Help me seize the day and praise You whenever I can!

THREE DAYS WITHOUT A MIRACLE

So the people grumbled against Moses, saying,
"What are we to drink?"
EXODUS 15:24 NIV

The Israelites were thirsty. Really, really thirsty. The kind of thirsty where they couldn't think of anything *but* water. Their tongues felt thick and their eyes burned under the relentless glare of the hot sun.

They had been wandering in the desert for three days without water, and they were about to snap. Could anyone blame them? Three million people, wandering in the desert without a road map, lacking such basic supplies as food and water. They did what people do when under stress. They blamed their leader. "Moses!" they complained. "It's all your fault!"

In reality, the Israelites had gone three days without a miracle. A few days prior, the Lord had parted the Red Sea, allowing the Israelites to escape, then closed it up again to drown the pursuing Egyptian army. Just three days ago! How had they forgotten God's just-in-time provision?

Moses didn't forget. His first response was to turn to God. "Then Moses cried out to the LORD, and the LORD showed him a piece of wood. He threw it into the water, and the water became fit to drink" (Exodus 15:25 NIV).

God held the answer to the Israelites' basic needs. He responded to Moses' prayer immediately, as if He had just been waiting.

What if we turned to God immediately with our basic needs instead of waiting until the thirst set in? What if we remembered His faithfulness before—or better still, instead of—panicking? Most likely, we would have our fresh water sooner.

Lord, You are the supplier of my every need. Thank You for Your faithfulness.